INVISIBLE MEN

INVISIBLE MEN

A Contemporary Slave Narrative in the Era of Mass Incarceration

By
Flores A. Forbes

Foreword by Robin D. G. Kelley

SKYHORSE PUBLISHING

Skyhorse Publishing books may be purchased in bulk at special discounts for sales promotion, corporate gifts, fund-raising, or educational purposes. Special editions can also be created to specifications. For details, contact the Special Sales Department, Skyhorse Publishing, 307 West 36th Street, 11th Floor, New York, NY 10018 or info@skyhorsepublishing.com.

Skyhorse® and Skyhorse Publishing® are registered trademarks of Skyhorse Publishing, Inc.®, a Delaware corporation.

Visit our website at www.skyhorsepublishing.com.

10 9 8 7 6 5 4 3 2 1

Library of Congress Cataloging-in-Publication Data is available on file.

Cover design by Rain Saukas
Cover photo credit iStock

ISBN: 978-1-5107-1170-9
Ebook ISBN: 978-1-5107-1171-6

Printed in the United States of America

To those invisible men who are still striving to remove the stigma of incarceration. If I can do it you can too. Good luck.

Table of Contents

Foreword   ix

Introduction   xv

Chapter 1: Wolf by the Ear   1

Chapter 2: Freedom and Slavery   13

Chapter 3: Reclaim Your Name   21

Chapter 4: Getting Back to the World   29

Chapter 5: Work (that Works for You)   45

Chapter 6: Heroes and Ghosts   63

Chapter 7: Family   85

Chapter 8: Coworkers and Bosses   93

Chapter 9: Community   99

Chapter 10: Mental and Physical Health   113

Chapter 11: Becoming Visible Men   135

Chapter 12: What We Need   157

Conclusion and Suggestions   175

Foreword

Robin D. G. Kelley

> . . . when you have lived invisible as long as I have you develop a certain ingenuity.
> —Ralph Ellison, *Invisible Man* (1952)

The protagonist in Ralph Ellison's classic novel spent his prime years trying to become a respectable Negro leader and seeking to secure a place for himself within the social fabric of the United States. He begins his journey as the object of white fascination, blindly pummeling other black boys for the titillation of Jim Crow's white fathers, undergoing respectability of training at the local Negro college, and finally seeking America's embrace as the unwitting victim of white Communist machinations. Then once the veil is lifted, he realizes that he is invisible and seeks refuge underground.

Flores A. Forbes, on the other hand, had no such illusions. A black working-class kid growing up in San Diego, he learned from his first encounter with the police that while his humanity, his aspirations, his dreams may be invisible to the white world, his body is not. Like so many young people of his generation, he joined the Black Panther Party, not to seek America's embrace but to transform the country. He wanted an end to police violence, an end to all forms of racism, a decent education, decent housing, the right of black people to determine their own destiny. They set out to bring down the old America and build a new world. And in order to do that, sometimes they *had* to become invisible by going underground. Whereas Ellison's protagonist may have ended the story as a guerrilla, of sorts, this is where Forbes's story begins.

But the invisibility required for guerrilla warfare proved elusive. Instead, Forbes was caught, convicted, and caged for four years, eight months, and nine days, initiating a different kind of invisibility. It began during his fugitive days prior to his incarceration and lasted well after his release, in the ongoing struggle to make a life for himself in the United States of America. Indeed, it is in the struggle for "re-entry," the heart of his modern-day "slave narrative," that Forbes's life most paralleled that of Ellison's *Invisible Man*, but shorn of all naive illusions.

To be clear, Forbes is not claiming that the conditions he endured are the same as antebellum chattel slavery. Slavery is invoked here as an analogy, a metaphor, a recurring nightmare. He did not have to pick cotton or cut cane, and despite the widespread use of prison labor, the joint does not carry the global economic weight of the plantation. Rather, he is talking about warehousing people, slavery by bureaucratic means. Forbes describes the vast machine that processes, houses, controls, and surveils the captured even after he is released. One striking parallel with chattel slavery is how the system made the entire black community vulnerable to surveillance and re-enslavement. Those who escaped slavery by *exercising their own free will* to resist their kidnapping were called fugitives. That one word rendered the vast majority of "free" black people in the antebellum period criminals on the lam for having committed grand theft larceny by stealing themselves away. And, lest we forget, an entire state and federal edifice was constructed and maintained to hunt down these thieves and bring them back to their masters. Justice had nothing to do with freedom; it was about protecting the master's property rights.[1]

Forbes knows what it means to be a fugitive, to be the target of the state. The Panthers were part of a larger

---

1 Why we cage over 2.5 million people in this country, and why the prison population grew exponentially since the late 1970s is beyond the scope of my little essay, nor is it the subject of Forbes's very personal and moving journey. There is much written on the subject, some of the best accounts include Ruth Wilson Gilmore, *Golden Gulag: Prisons, Surplus, Crisis, and Opposition in Globalizing California* (Los Angeles and Berkeley: University of California Press, 2007); Elizabeth Hinton, *From the War on Poverty to the War on Crime: The Making of Mass Incarceration in America* (Cambridge, Mass.: Harvard University Press, 2016); Michelle Alexander, *The New Jim Crow: Mass Incarceration in the Age of Colorblindness* (New York: The New Press, 2012).

insurgency—against police violence, racism, poverty, war in Vietnam and elsewhere—that was ultimately put down through state repression and massive surveillance. The men and women caught up in this dragnet became "political prisoners," whether they violated the law or were simply convicted on the flimsiest of evidence. Political prisoners are not relics from the past; many are serving time now or were only recently released. Many Americans are familiar with Mumia Abu Jamal and the exiled Assata Shakur, or might be vaguely familiar with the tragic life of Albert Woodfox, but very few know the names Abdullah Majid, Jalil Muntaqim, Sundiata Acoli, Jamil Al-Amin, Herman Bell, Veronza Bowers, Romaine "Chip" Fitzgerald, Patrice Lumumba Ford, Robert "Seth" Hayes, Mumia Abu-Jamal, Mondo we Langa, Ruchelle "Cinque" Magee, Hugo Pinell, Ed Poindexter, Kamau Sadiki, Dr. Mutulu Shakur, Russell "Maroon" Shoatz, Sekou Abdullah Odinga, and Susan Rosenberg.

And yet, Forbes resists the tendency to distinguish "political prisoners" from the general population serving time for crimes ranging from drug possession and parole violations to burglary and murder. He doesn't fall into the trap of separating out the "deserving" inmate from the undeserving, the revolutionary hero from the thug. The truth is, the system throws up barriers to all formerly incarcerated people trying to find a way forward. While the organization and discipline he learned from the Panthers proved immensely helpful, he confronted many obstacles for which he was not prepared.

Forbes's story of reentry is really several parallel stories that occasionally collide, creating moments of disorientation and explosive possibility. In his quest for freedom, he recognizes that "Invisible men" and women must navigate behind invisible bars—barriers to employment, housing, even the right to vote. And his past as a Panther never goes away; it inspires and haunts him relentlessly. And yet, like most slave narratives, not everyone he encounters is evil or hostile. It may seem disconcerting to some readers to learn about his supportive professors, how he succeeded at San Jose State writing critically and freely, enjoying a life of the mind to which few people who have never served a day in jail don't always have access.

Yes, Forbes prevails in the end, but don't be fooled. The point of this modern-day slave narrative is neither to produce another Horatio Alger myth, to titillate with gruesome stories of abject violence, to scare kids "straight" so they don't choose a life a crime, nor to merely propose a raft of reforms. Rather, it is a provocation for all of us to see the invisible men and women who must navigate a system that is unsustainable, degrading, and racist. To bring these men and women into visibility is to make the prison disappear.

Introduction

"I was looking for myself and asking everyone except myself questions which I, and only I, could answer. It took me a long time and much painful boomeranging of my expectations to achieve a realization everyone else appears to have been born with: That I am nobody but myself."

—Ralph Ellison, *Invisible Man*

I was an invisible man. I was rendered invisible in my teens by society—black, male, working-class poor. I was invisible by choice as a member of the Black Panther Party (BPP), fighting to lift up all black people, everyone a victim of racial, class, and gender inequality. I was invisible by choice, living and hiding from the authorities. I was invisible against my will in prison. I wanted to be visible, and since my release from incarceration, I've become that—a free, self-determined, functional, and thriving human being. The work I had to do to achieve this has been worth it. I want other invisible men to know that it is possible to want to be seen in the world and in the mirror.

The best scene in Ralph Ellison's classic novel, *Invisible Man*, is when the unnamed protagonist bumps into a white man and the unnamed protagonist becomes irate and demands the reason for the white man invading his space. The white man responds, "I am sorry but I did not see you."

I was in prison shuttered away out of sight for no one to see. I was serving time for attempting to kill a witness who was testifying against Huey P. Newton, the founder of the Black Panther Party. The operation was botched, and one of us was killed by friendly fire. I was wounded and fled, turning myself in three years later. I was subsequently convicted of felony murder and sentenced to eight years in the California Department of Corrections. I served four years, eight months, and nine days. Upon my release I was determined to continue helping my people but in a different way and within the system. I finished college and graduate school, becoming a successful urban planning executive, city planner, and a university administrator at an Ivy League institution in New York City. During my professional practice I created thousands of jobs, provided technical assistance to thousands of small businesses, built thousands of affordable housing units, and planned and implemented a major revitalization in Harlem, New York City. The journey after prison was not easy, as I was a victim of the stigma of incarceration. The stigma of incarceration caused me to conceal my past for fifteen years, rendering me by choice an invisible man.

I never thought about the concept of invisibility as a black man until I read Ralph Ellison's novel for a literature class I was taking while serving time at Soledad State Prison in Salinas, California. I read the book twice, having so much time to commit to reading books, and as the concept of invisibility and the imagery of a black man not being recognized in plain sight fascinated me.

Equally, the invisibility we experience as incarcerated black men has somewhat of a dual nature here in prison and on the outside. The more typical experience for a black man who is incarcerated is that you are gone and most people who may know you realize they have not seen you for a while. I am sure many of us on the local and neighborhood level have experienced this at local barbershops, as one of these disappeared men walks in the door and everyone is surprised to see him again. "Man, where have you been?" he is asked. "Up north," or "Upstate," he responds. Or sometimes he just says, "I was down for a count in such and such joint."

On the other hand, when you have been invisible in this way, it also reflects your sense of the world on a personal level with regard to culture, style, technology, and other basic changes as the world turns without you knowing it. I was physically invisible to the world from 1980 to 1985, and there is so much I was not familiar with during that period. Even today I can't pinpoint the date of certain songs, movies, and other cultural shifts that took place while I was away up north. I missed the rise of Michael Jackson as a solo artist, in particular his breakout album *Off the Wall*. From the joint I saw Michael Jordan make the shot that defeated Georgetown in the NCAA Championship, but he still remained unfamiliar to me prior to my release. And I missed the release of *Scarface* starring Al Pacino, one of my favorite actors.

I realized I was not in plain sight of anyone outside of the prison, as I had also lost my identity as a human being. The name my parents Fred and Catherine Forbes gave me meant nothing for the first time in my life. My name had been replaced by a number: C-72851. Prior to this, however, I did experience what it was like to disappear of my own volition. I was a fugitive for three years, and this caused me to miss the news that my father had died two years before I surrendered.

Sadly today, the imprint of that number is so powerful that I still remember my C number by memory, just like I remember my social security number. I am sure that many other formerly incarcerated people experience the same. So, like our ancestors who were brought to these shores in chains as slaves and subsequently lost their given names from Africa to the Americanized names of their slave owners, I too, like others, was a nameless slave. For me this imagery of being invisible in prison is like being in a cave, in the wilderness, a fugitive on the run, or woodshedding like a comic, practicing my material before I stand up in front of an audience and make them laugh. Many of us have thought for long hours what it would be like to emerge from our cave or prison cell and return to the world. It was frightening for me at first and then became traumatic when I heard a "lifer" I was playing chess with talk about getting out and being free.

The brother had gotten a release date and was soon to be free. I, on the other hand, was concentrating on my next two or three moves and was focusing on the board, when I looked up and saw he was staring at me with serious but glassy eyes. No one stares at another person in prison, unless you know them well, or you are trying to send an unhealthy and menacing message, or you want someone's attention, as he wanted mine. I asked him why he was look-ing at me like that, and he said, "Brother Forbes, you have been in the joint a few years, and I have been down for fif-teen years. What's it like out there?"

I thought for a few seconds and grasped that this was an important moment in his life, so I toppled my king in sur-render and said, "This is important, so let's just end the game." He said, "Cool." I said, "Brother Man, I cannot tell you what it will be like for you because I don't know what it's going to be like for me. And until you asked me this, I was not thinking about getting out but was paying more attention to surviving in this place."

He was released on the date assigned, and as many of us would do, we were assembled near the gate as he left for Soledad Central to be released. He shook my hand and said thanks for the advice, and as we hugged, he said in my ear, "I am scared to death." My release date was coming soon, and I wondered if I was going to feel the same way he did.

The preparation for getting out of prison has to start the moment you go in, that is, after the shock of one's confinement wears off and you begin to program your life for reentry. You must rely on help from outside the institution, on your personal efforts at preparing yourself skill-wise, and on assistance from loved ones. Even with all of that, you really don't know what lies ahead for you beyond these walls, so you are actually in the dark. Therefore, an incarcerated person's vision to the outside world is pretty much distorted. People who are in prison serving time have no right or perceived rationale to guide those about to be released from prison and should never be giving advice to a fellow inmate about the outside world. Even though it happens all the time.

On the other hand, and even less fruitful, is the advice one may get from the institutional counselors, guards, and other so-called prison advisors whom you meet with during pre-release. Advice from anyone in this group of people borders on insanity or more like a slaveholder from the antebellum period giving advice to a freed slave about how he should conduct himself as a free man in a slaveholding society.

*　*　*

I have often thought about this brother and the other black men I met in prison and wondered about how they did once emancipated. The "lifer" was frightened because he had become acclimated, or institutionalized, to the penitentiary, and in the harsh reality of this godforsaken place, every incarcerated person acclimates, adjusts. He had to survive in the present condition. We have to adjust again when we're given our lives back. He had become contented with his invisibility and the permanence of the endless programming that one encounters with the constant ringing of the Pavlovian-type bells, your A, B, or C number, the death that lurks around any cell block corner, and the trigger-happy bulls that sit in the mess hall gun cages or peer down at you from the gun towers in the yard. This same fear haunted me, as being in prison was nothing like being an invisible person on the street. Just the thought of walking out of these gates gave me pause. I had so much trepidation because when I was to be released, I had no idea of what I would encounter on the outside.

Ellison's construct of invisibility focused on black Americans being irrelevant and relegated as just part of the furniture in the master's house, covered with sheets in the American landscape of white supremacy. So much so, they have been rendered invisible.

In prison you are invisible from society, and once the prison gates are thrown open for you, that cloak of invisibility will remain if you don't do something positive to move your life forward. Or, in the words of Ellison's protagonist in *Invisible Man*, "Perhaps that's my greatest social crime, I've overstayed my hibernation, since there's a possibility that even an invisible man has a socially responsible role to play."

I am now fully prepared to remove the cloak of invisibility and be seen as a human being completely emancipated and restored.

CHAPTER 1

Wolf by the Ear

"But, as it is, we have the **wolf by the ear**, and we can neither hold him, nor safely let him go. Justice is in one scale, and self-preservation in the other."
—Thomas Jefferson to John Holmes,
Monticello, 22 April 1820

The wolf-by-the-ear quote is from a letter Thomas Jefferson wrote to John Holmes about the pending legislation regarding slavery and how it was being regulated state by state that became the Missouri Compromise. To me, Jefferson was quite clear about his attitude toward slaves and their presence in his country and that if there was a general emancipation, expatriation must follow quickly. That is the only way to release the wolf's ear, his elegant metaphor for slavery. The issue

1

of slavery and mass incarceration go hand in hand as they are coupled constitutionally at the hip within the Thirteenth Amendment. Jefferson did not believe in emancipation without expulsion from America, and many in today's society do not believe black men who have been to prison should walk the same streets as they do. But if they do walk the same streets, many believe this should only happen with limitations to their freedom. In addition to the Thirteenth Amendment, which makes you a slave if convicted of a crime and sentenced to prison, there are many more obstacles once you are released. There are various laws, public statutes, and specific occupational hiring restrictions, disenfranchisement as well as parole. When black men are released, they have another strike against them: the fact that they are black and historically oppressed and still seamlessly connected to the peculiar institution of slavery.

Loïc Wacquant targets this historical perspective brilliantly in his 2002 article in the *New Left Review,* "From Slavery to Mass Incarceration." Slavery up to the Civil War made the free labor of African Americans the foundation of the American economy. After slavery, it was Jim Crow, establishing as it did legal racial apartheid to support an economy based on agriculture. The civil rights movement broke that system, but in its place emerged urban ghettos outside the South, "corresponding to conjoint urbanization and proletarianization of African Americans from the Great Migration of 1914–30 to the 1960s . . . slavery and mass incarceration are genealogically linked and that one

2

cannot understand the latter—its timing, composition and smooth onset as well as the quiet ignorance or acceptance of its deleterious effects on those it affects—without returning to the former as historic starting point."

So apparently, according to Wacquant, Jefferson's elegant metaphor for slavery has transformed into the carceral state of today.

Nevertheless, one must adjust to the reality of prison as one must adjust again to the reality out of prison. The newly released black man is an invisible man due to his incarceration, but will remain invisible by choice until he overcomes the stigma of that experience.

August 9, 1985, I was released from the California Department of Corrections (CDC) after serving four years, eight months, and nine days for felony murder. I used a gun against someone. That was thirty-plus years ago, and now I have a nice life: meaningful work, a wife, a family, and my health.

I did my time under the guise of a political prisoner, but that means something only in prison, not in society. Upon release, I was a black man with two felony convictions, a prison term, and no record of having had a job; I was thirty-three years old. I am a part of a group of black men without a constituency or advocate and all but invisible in this society. That group is black men in America who have served their time and not gone back to prison. Most of us are invisible by choice and will not reveal ourselves. We cannot because of the stigma attached to being formerly incarcerated.

Mainstream media, and even scholars, talk a lot about the recidivism rate and the disproportionate sentencing of black men by the courts. They don't spend enough time talking about people who don't return to jail—the people who remain free, work, and contribute to society after serving their sentences. The formerly incarcerated are an understudied population. Today the recidivism rate is around 65 percent. We need to pay attention and do the work of lowering that rate down to zero. But, we can't continue to neglect people who make an effort to stay out of the criminal justice system. The ones who don't get hooked on being locked up—the 35 percent who don't go back, especially black men. It is they who have been a primary target of this country's history of selective discrimination against nonwhites in general and the formerly incarcerated in particular. According to the NAACP's *Criminal Justice Fact Sheet*, one in six black men had been incarcerated as of 2001. If current trends continue, one in three black males born today can expect to spend time in prison.

One of the reasons why I fared well since my release from incarceration was I had a vision and a plan to reinvent myself. Even before prison I had spent eighteen years completely in hiding from the authorities, off the grid of a normal life. I chose that life because I felt the reasons why I was an outlaw were justified.

As a young black man growing up in Southern California, I, along with my peer group, was terrorized by the police. We often spoke about what to do and one day we saw what two black men were doing in Oakland, California. Huey P. Newton and Bobby Seale had started an organization called the Black Panther Party, and one of their first efforts was to patrol police with guns and law books in an attempt to end police brutality and the murder of black people. At the age of sixteen, I joined and spent the next ten years fighting for my people. I believed deeply in what we were fighting for, so deeply I embraced the most radical of our internal beliefs. We believed, as did most sovereign states and other revolutionary movements, that violence was a policy instrument. I was recruited into the Panther military unit after several years of service.

My work in this section of the party was mostly in the underground as well. I was part of a group within the BPP that provided protection to our leaders as well as doing covert work in the streets against our various enemies. I was also the Black Panther Party armorer, or, if you use the regular, more traditional military term, I was the quartermaster who acquired, stored, and maintained the arsenal of weapons we had collected over the years. In 1977, I, along with two of my comrades, attempted to kill a witness who was testifying against Huey P. Newton. The operation was botched: friendly fire killed one of my comrades and I was wounded. Friendly fire is when you and your comrades accidentally shoot one another. If someone is killed during the commission of a felony, everyone involved who lives can be charged with felony murder. I was involved and survived to live another day and went underground. I remained a fugitive for three years. I turned myself in of my own volition in 1980 and was eventually convicted of felony murder. I was sentenced to eight years.

While in prison, I read and studied and took college courses, using a Pell grant. While at Soledad State Prison, I enrolled in a college-degree program being run by San José State University. Once completed, I could receive a bachelor's degree in Interdisciplinary Studies of the Social Sciences. The professors were all full-time faculty from this California state university, and they taught courses in psychology, sociology, American literature, statistics, philosophy, and the capstone course for the degree, the Social Sciences Seminar. In the California Department of Corrections, once you started serious programming, your schedule involved one week of work (I was a tutor who taught life skills to the inmates), and an education week, filled with classes from SJSU.

The life-skills classes I taught were very depressing. I worked with mostly black inmates who could barely read. It was troublesome to me to hold up a flash card with the word *truck* on one side and the only way the inmates would discover what the word was was when I flipped the card to its reverse side to reveal the photograph of a truck. But I was finding my real self and developing a plan during the week of my education program.

There were about thirty inmates taking the bachelor of arts (BA) courses. About five were black, maybe ten were white, and the balance was Chicanos and Pacific Islanders. It was fabulous taking these classes, but one had to pay attention during these periods as half of the white guys were part of the Aryan Brotherhood, which was the Nazi gang in the joint. Their remarks about Boers and other racist bullshit made me keep one eye on my coursework and the other on them. Nevertheless, I began to understand that this intense coursework was part of my process of reinvention, which was not unfamiliar to me as a black person in this country.

I remembered how my father and mother shifted their lives from a segregated, nondescript, working-class livelihood to a middle-class livelihood. They were hard working and good, churchgoing black people. My father, who I loved dearly, taught me good lessons as a black man in America. He used to tell me and my siblings not to take shit from anyone and that you should never feel sorry for a white person as they have never given a shit about you. Sadly, my father who was a great believer in education did not live long enough to experience my educational achievements. He died of a heart attack while I was a fugitive. That was the saddest moment of my life. For a while my family believed I was dead. But I shocked them all when I resurfaced and turned myself in. My mother was the only immediate family member who visited me in prison, along with two girlfriends, Frances and Veronica. My mother was a real trooper, as she sent me care packages of cigarettes, coffee, and other sweets that we called zoo zoos and wham whams.

I studied self-hypnosis in an attempt to devise a plan to help myself. I do not remember the name of the book, but it basically taught you to think deeply enough to believe you had put yourself in a trance. Once in the trance you were supposed to make positive suggestions to yourself, like *I will get a good job and make some money.* I used to chant that once I got out I was going to stay out. I read books that could help me redirect my life. *Think and Grow Rich,* by Napoleon Hill, was the most useful and helped me draw a road map for my life once I was freed. I followed all of his steps to success, such as developing a plan and writing it out. Each day you were supposed to read your plan and devise other steps to success, like finding other types of support going forward, like creating a mastermind group comprised of a network of advisors within the field of one's choice.

My plan once released was to finish college, go to graduate school, and become a professional urban planner. I decided to become an urban planner because I saw many similarities between my years in the BPP doing community development work and the work that urban planners do. They are in a position to plan and reshape communities, towns, and cities and create better environments for people. That's what I wanted to do. So, I became determined to find a way to do that.

Release from incarceration frees you from a concrete and metal box, but as a result, if you need a job once you are out, another form of oppression excludes you from obtaining that job. That is the "Box." The question that all formerly incarcerated people dread: Have you ever been convicted of a felony? It's there to torture and bar you even if the literal metal box is not there. If yes is your truth, then you've got some explaining to do: the date, type of offense, docket number, etc., associated with this felony charge. Today, however, over one hundred municipalities and some states and federal employers have banned the Box. But in the early days of my freedom, it was, and still is in many instances, rigorously applied. But even with progressive reforms looking to open things up, the real issue is the attitude of the hiring manager who believes you are as guilty of your crime as you were when you were incarcerated and should be punished for the balance of your life.

Follow the advice of the literature, such as the book *What Color Is Your Parachute?* and you'll answer yes. They advise that if you then get an interview, you can explain. Well, in my experience and as in the experience of many others, that is not the move. When I checked "Yes," it seemed an invisible hand would come out from under the table and yank the job application out of my hands, flinging it into the trash bin. When I was lucky enough to get an interview, I followed the book's advice when the interviewer asked, "Is there anything else you would like to tell us that is not on your résumé?" Well, I'd truthfully and fully answer and that would also quickly end the interview. I finally took another approach: for years I just flat-out lied. Those in the know called it being job smart, especially if the company was not doing a background check.

Everyone deserves a second chance, or else the idea of serving your time and paying your debt to society is bullshit. The reality is that your indebtedness, or rather your punishment, damn near never ends. I was felony-free for fifteen years and had a bachelor's and master's degree in urban planning. And yet I had to work my way through the secondary labor force in New York City because of the Box. That means I did menial labor at very low wages and with scant benefits that one did not receive until after a period of probation. My goal was to enter the primary labor force, which included salaried jobs with real benefits that you received the day you signed your hiring letter.

My luck didn't change for the better until I found an NYC Department of Investigation (DOI) investigator who trusted and understood me, and knew something about urban American history.

You reach points when you feel stuck and in a rut. I began to feel that way. As I was working my way through the workforce system of New York City as an urban planner, I discovered that working in the public sector was a better pathway to success. Otherwise, you can find yourself relegated to low-level and low-paying positions that lead to a dead end. The ideal position in the field of urban planning is to get a high-level policy job within NYC's public sector, where one is dealing with the NYC Zoning Resolution, land use–zoning and interacting with architects and engineers developing brick and mortar projects in and around NYC. This kind of position brings you into contact with real estate developers, financial intermediaries, and other movers and shakers shaping the streets and skyline of New York City.

An opportunity presented itself for me to move closer to where I wanted to be. A friend of mine from graduate school came to see me one day at work. He was working with the Manhattan Borough president, C. Virginia Fields, and said they were looking for someone to head up planning and development efforts in Harlem. He said he thought I had the chops for the job and asked that I consider applying for it.

There would be a background check, but he assured me that being open and honest about my past would not pose a problem. I was the best-qualified person he said, and that's all that mattered. The New York City Department of Investigation wanted everything on the application except blood, a urine sample, and semen. I was fingerprinted twice, once for the state and again for the FBI. They did a credit check, income tax review, and wanted to know every address I had lived at for the past ten years. As I went through the grueling application process, the borough president's general counsel kept reminding me: "tell the truth, that's what counts." She was right and I was hired.

After four months on the job, I got a call from the New York City Department of Investigation. The investigator on the phone from DOI said, "We just got the last of your FBI information back from your fingerprints." He paused for a moment. I could hear him breathing as he said, "Mr. Forbes, you have eight major felony arrests, two felony convictions, and one prison term, can I ask what in the hell were you doing?"

I said, "I was in the Black Panther Party for ten years."

He laughed and said, "Oh, okay, now let's talk about your taxes."

CHAPTER 2

Freedom and Slavery

"Neither slavery nor involuntary servitude, except as a punishment for crime whereof the party shall have been duly convicted, shall exist within the United States, or any place subject to their jurisdiction."
— Amendment XIII, Section 1, US Constitution

The Thirteenth Amendment to the United States Constitution did two contradictory things at the same time: making slavery illegal on one hand and making slavery legal as a punishment for a crime on the other hand. This classic white supremacist loophole, so to speak, opened the door to continuing the enslavement of people by criminalizing them, particularly the black and poor.

In his classic book *Black Reconstruction*, W. E. B. Du Bois writes about the slave following Emancipation, saying, "The slave went free; stood a brief moment in the sun; then moved back again toward slavery." The day I left prison was the brightest day of my life, as much as it is with most black men who've served time in prison. That's when you understand the value of freedom because you know from experience what it means to be enslaved. We're not always ready for the freedom we seek, but as human beings regardless, we deserve it. The bright moment can also leave a man newly released from incarceration feeling lost and befuddled. Finding your place in society again is hard. Finding your place in a society that had categorized you as property, forced your labor, held you against your will, and tortured you is a Herculean task.

It was believed by slave owners in antebellum times that the enslaved couldn't flourish and survive as freed-men without their help. They believed we were incapable of running our own lives, to justify their desire to control us. Chattel slavery ended, but the enslavement of men has continued in new forms. One of the major forms of slavery today is imprisonment: the prison industrial complex. After Emancipation the future shock of the Thirteenth Amendment's "exception clause" brought many black men back into various forms of servitude. There was the prison leasing system that was set up to enslave black men, who were in many cases unjustly convicted of a crime, and once incarcerated, their services were leased out to various contractors. Many of these contractors were former slave owners. Similarly, the Black Codes, a form of long-tailed parole, confined many black people beyond the bars by taking away any civil rights they thought they had by excluding them from participating on juries or owning property or a business, and making it illegal for them to ever testify against a white person. So many black people after Emancipation were relegated to a segregated lifestyle of squalor and poverty with no rights at all.

Mass media and popular culture have promoted images of the black man as a boogeyman, a hulking creature, and a menace to society. A police report after an arrest in 1974 described me as innately intelligent in a spooky or mystical way. I refused to cooperate and respond to their questions without a lawyer present. They wrote, "[We can't look at him because] his eyes seem to be peeking inside our brains." More broadly, I recall the stories of my male relatives and my fellow Black Panthers, Army grunts in Vietnam during the war. The white US soldiers told the Vietnamese that all black men grow tails when they reach the age of twenty-one. My cousin said while he was being serviced by a prostitute in Saigon that she kept looking at his butt curiously. He asked her what was the problem, and she pointed and asked, "Where is black man's tail?"

These examples, while ludicrous and insulting, are not as damaging as the way white society has cast the black man as the poster boy for criminality. Khalil Muhammad, in *The Condemnation of Blackness*, discusses how "blackness" became "the singular mark of a criminal." The Federal Bureau of Investigation's report titled *Uniform Crime Reports* bears this out. Or even earlier in the twentieth century in *An American Dilemma*, Nobel Laureate Gunnar

Myrdal writes about racial beliefs in the United States as "[t]he beliefs in the Negro's inborn laziness and thriftlessness, his happy-go-lucky nature, his lack of morals, his criminal tendencies . . ." And Loïc Wacquant expands the conversation in this space when he states, "[T]he expansion and intensification of the activities of the police, courts, and prison over the past quarter-century have been finely targeted by class, ethnicity, and place, leading to what is better referred to as the hyper-incarceration of one particular category: lower-class black men in the crumbling ghetto."

Doing time is hard, but basically what you did to take care of yourself was mind your own fucking business in the joint. You can get used to that. Guys in prison come back repeatedly because they can't figure out how to be a regular Joe who isn't involved in any criminal activity. You have to plan your life in order to stay out of places like prison once you have been released. I know this may sound rather contradictory, coming from me, because it was my street planning of urban guerilla tactics that got me locked up in the first place. The dissembling, lying, and shifting, where one must lie about who one is and where one has been, or the construction of a false identity so that one can fly under the radar so as to not be detected, is stressful and agonizing. Many people who do not have criminal backgrounds do this as they fabricate much of their résumé in order to qualify for certain jobs. Well, now I was going to use that ability to stay out and rebuild my young life. I was trained at dissembling, developing new identities, and moving about the streets and society in stealth. This all really proved helpful for the three years I was a fugitive on the run. During that time I used two different names and identities as I worked my way across the country for three years. I was John Wesley Tate and Carl Tribble from 1977 to 1980.

Anyway, the case in point, with regard to guys staying out, getting visibility, finding or not finding freedom, is this. Traditionally, when your time is short—about thirty days before release—you are placed in what's called pre-release status. This makes you eligible to follow a program to prepare yourself for release. They offer "life-skills" classes, Adult Basic Education (ABE), and stuff like that. It's a quick fix. I didn't take any of that stuff that they wanted me to, because I believed I was ready to go. But most of the brothers are not. An example of this is one brother who was on pre-release status with me who is probably more typical of young men that are in prison. He had been down for about eighteen months on a three-year sentence this time. He had been incarcerated before. We were walking the yard together with a few other brothers. And the topic of conversation, as usual, was about getting out. I was explaining my own three-point program. I had said as much before: 1. Get my BA; 2. Find a job to hold me over; 3. Get my advanced degree to open the door to more lucrative opportunities. They were probably tired of hearing that shit, but too bad. I listened to them. They had to listen to me. Besides, I had a reputation they wanted, and because of that, they respected me or at least respected what I used to be. The brother who's getting out, on the same day as me, starts to tell us what his plans are.

"Well, when I get out next month or when my date gets here, this is what I'm gonna do. First, I'm gonna catch that dog [Greyhound Bus] back to the Bay Area. Go see my parole officer and collect my $100.00 and then test for drugs. After that, I'm gonna go see the dope man and get fixed up, you know. Then, I'm gonna take a few days off and plan what I'm gonna do for the rest of my life."

Damn, I said to myself, I gotta get as far away from this nigga as possible. Talk and thinking like that scared me. I could tell he was definitely coming back.

But what was even more frightening was my own "self" discovery of how unprepared I was for life in the world not only before release, but before I joined the Black Panther Party—way back then. I had a lot to learn. Most of us do. And, one of the important lessons is that being in prison makes you an integral part of the system in the deepest and truest sense.

The C-number you receive in prison replaces your name and forever haunts you with its negative connotation. My number was C-72851. Thirty years after the fact, I know it like people know their phone numbers or Social Security numbers.

You really don't begin to understand this society, or the system, until you encounter or engage it, at its many different levels of interaction. Just imagine: this country has been organizing unopposed for over two hundred years. That's an awesome thought when you seriously consider it alongside the other lightweight countries in the world, you know. And this brother wants to plan for three days and then talk shit about how the system is against him and his, and how black people are never gonna get a fair shake until somebody backs down and gives them something. Bullshit.

But now, I was hip to what this society and its systems were really about. They had been changing rules, definitions, and categories to benefit them and oppress us. They had enslaved us, and when forced to emancipate us, came up with a way to sabotage that. They then criminalized us to justify another form of enslavement. I had encountered this society and its systems on almost every level of interaction, and now I knew what it would take to get mine, or at least I believed I did. I had been a naive young black man, who put to memory his social security number, which systematically branded me. I had been a black revolutionary, who put to memory the Ten-Point Platform and Program of the Black Panther Party. And as a result of hard work, I rose up through the ranks and became a shot caller, and then I put to memory the tenets of the Buddha Samurai. (This was Huey P. Newton's street innovation that engendered esprit de corps within the ranks of the soldiers in the party.) I had been a fugitive and had seen the underbelly of this system, and put to memory my list of aliases. And now I was inside the system, and could see its intestines. And then I really became aware of the danger I was in. Having been swallowed up in its judicial system was enough warning for me. I would have to get serious about what it would take to get out and stay out and then to build, and eventually lead a productive life once I was out. So I studied it; I read about it; I talked to my professors in here about it; and I collected my thoughts and planned my move.

I had locked and loaded new ammunition in my brand new weapon—my mind. That new ammunition was education. My new weapon: a steeled brain, rehabilitated, refreshed, and capable of handling any complex idea or problem that existed. And it was all tempered with the patience and humbleness of a newly restored citizen who wants to maintain his status as a formerly incarcerated black man who will never return to prison.

CHAPTER 3

Reclaim Your Name

"A man dressed in black appeared, a long-haired fellow whose piercing eyes looked down upon me out of an intense and friendly face. The others hovered about him, their eyes anxious as he alternately peered at me and consulted my chart. Then he scribbled something on a large card and thrust it before my eyes.

WHAT IS YOUR NAME?"

—Ralph Ellison, *Invisible Man*

When you are in prison, regardless of race and gender, you lose your parent-given name to the state or federal number you become classified by. This affects people in different ways. For me I became angry and determined to recover my name and thereby reclaim my life as a human being. I badly wanted to be seen again.

Once a formerly incarcerated black man has decided to be seen, his work in earnest to reenter society has begun. The real process of rehabilitation, or assimilating into society, can only take place once you have been freed and progress out of parole or probation. Parole can be onerous for many, as most formerly incarcerated people have a name for being supervised outside of the wall: the tail. It follows you once you have been released from the actual prison and can wrap its tentacles around your neck and choke you to death if you are not careful. It can affect your job prospects, especially if your parole officer is a dick. I was told a story by a formerly incarcerated friend that he was violated and sent back to prison because his parole officer would not adjust his schedule so that he could take a certain job. The request was made by this brother and his parole officer refused. Well, this is my analysis of the parole system and the parole officer. The more successful the returning citizen is, the more irrelevant the parole officer becomes as his or her caseload dwindles. It's not unusual to hear a parole officer refer to the clients in their caseload as "my people."

The path to reentry can be an arduous process. Especially if you didn't begin envisioning who you want to be and where you want to go in life and develop a plan— thirty days before release or more. But, even if you did, as boxer Mike Tyson said, "Everyone that enters the ring has a plan, until they get hit."

You have to be prepared to take some punches, not physically, but mentally and emotionally. So, check your mental and emotional state. Reflect on how you're feeling. Are you sad? Hopeful? Angry? Do you have someone you trust to talk to as you walk the gauntlet? At this point one needs a support network that is not connected to the parole system. You need something like a coach or mentor to help you through the early phase of emancipation. Some embrace faith. Christianity is one belief system that many convert to while in prison, and they pray that it will guide them to successful reentry once released. However, many black men convert to Islam while in the joint and find their way to a supportive masjid once on the streets. Now, today becoming a Muslim in prison is one way to connect with a support group, which can help you once you are released, but this can be risky. Given the Islamophobia in America, it can be risky inside, as you will probably be under surveillance, which will enhance that long parole tail once released. But for me I found support in my plan and loved ones. But no support group is more important than you being determined and focused on reclaiming your name and identity as a tax-paying and hardworking returning citizen.

Black men in particular must develop skills and learn the tools to create and identify the steps they need to follow. They must take these steps in order to sustain a life in America. Fifteen years felony-free is a reasonable time for the process to be completed. Some may complete the cycle sooner, but I propose it takes an average of at least fifteen years to see the fruits of your work. Your primary goal is to remove the stigma of incarceration, which is what really affects your name and identity as a person.

The early steps might be working in the secondary labor force: an entry-level job, physical labor, minimum wage, and little or no benefits. Early on after release and while I was still in college, I worked casual labor in Berkeley. I worked for a company that bought used office furniture and then resold it. This was hard, back-breaking work, but as I said you need to get back into the groove of work and life by being determined to reenter the workforce at any level. Your goal and aspiration might be to move from the secondary labor force into the primary labor force to a salaried position in the professional and producer services industries.

I was focused on being a professional urban planner, but others can make their way by taking other paths. I have found that many brothers have become barbers. One in particular that I know has become a successful entre-preneur, having learned his craft in prison. He has been out of prison for over twenty-five years, giving back and contributing to the economy and the community by making jobs available for other formerly incarcerated men who have also taken up that trade. He has reclaimed his name and also removed the stigma of incarceration and is very visible as a restored citizen in the Village of Harlem today.

Life experience in the Black Panther Party was a great learning and supportive resource for me. I saw myself as a soldier fighting a war of liberation and as an individual I was determined to survive. Going to prison and reentering society was just one of many consequences for this lifestyle. Huey P. Newton once told me that the party would eventually be destroyed, because we were challenging a mighty nation and that the revolution might not be successful. But your goal should you survive is to organize your life to continue the struggle by other means. So what was important once I was out of prison was to carry on my struggle by some other process. For me, that was becoming a professional urban planner—a field, as I saw it, that would make me much more effective at helping my people at this stage of my journey.

But two Harvard researchers, Bruce Western and Devah Pager, have done extensive work in this space, and some of their results can give a black man pause with attempting to get employment after a prison term, and even more so for just being a black man without a criminal background trying to find meaningful work. Professor Western points out in his book *Punishment and Inequality in America* that "[a] prison record diverts ex-offenders from career jobs through its effects on skills, social connections, and the criminal stigma. The stigma of incarceration does not prohibit employment entirely. It simply limits entry into high-status or career jobs. Researchers have found that men in trusted or high-income occupations before conviction are unable to return to those positions." Professor Pager conducted an experiment using two sets of testers, one group of black men and another group of white men who applied for the same group of jobs. She discusses some of the findings in her book *Marked*: "In the present study, black job seekers presenting identical credentials to their white counterparts received callbacks from employers at less than half the rate of whites. Even more striking, the results show that even a black applicant with no criminal background fares no better—and perhaps worse—than does a white applicant with a felony conviction."

Moreover, Bruce Western has studied and written about the process of reentry and forthrightly states that if you are a black man coming out of prison, on parole, or on probation—if one has been encumbered by the criminal justice system in any way—this transition is nearly impossible. But he proposes three levels of attainment that a black man can aspire to and work toward—the steps:

1. Acquire skills and get experience using those skills. The system has a record of your interactions with the criminal justice system. Now you're establishing a record of how productive and capable you are in the workplace.
2. Find social networks to establish and maintain connections to people and sources that can help you.
3. Learn the psychological and other tools to overcome the STIGMA of a criminal conviction, prison term, and encumbrance of the criminal justice system. The more positive and confident you are, the more you'll receive that back from others.

Over the past thirty years, I have overcome all three levels of attainment to reentry, as have many other black men. But how did I do this with the odds set against me?

CHAPTER 4

Getting Back to the World

"America is the land of the second chance—and when the gates of the prison open, the path ahead should lead to a better life."

—George W. Bush

I was lying on my bunk, listening to Luther Vandross's "Busy Body" on a Walkman I had borrowed from a brother in another dorm. It was August 9, 1985, around 3:00 a.m. I had been awake all night—damn. How could I sleep knowing that in about five hours they would begin to process me out of the California Department of Corrections. I was anxious. I had waited, and waited, and waited . . . four years, eight months, and nine days to be exact. I had taken responsibility for my actions. I had paid the price. I wanted my life back.

I was ready, completely rejuvenated and rehabilitated. These last hours were killing me inside. In a few hours I would experience the humiliation of prison life—the strip searches, with someone looking up your ass; the Pavlov's dog conditioning of those goddamn bells, one for lunch, two for showers, and three for lock-up—for the last time. I had had enough of this bullshit.

I had been building up my skill levels by reading, writing, and calculating every possible math problem I could. I had read every kind of book I could get my hands on. History books, American literature, Chinese literature, logic, philosophy, statistics and yes, Napoleon Hill's *Think and Grow Rich*. I read them all, and I planned my life, thinking as a free black man.

I nodded off at some point, hours before release. And it was the sunlight breaking through the windows of my dormitory that woke me up. It was time. I sprang to my feet, while clicking the Walkman eject button to remove the tape. I took the earphones off my head, grabbed my prison dress-outs, and bounced down to the showers for the last time. It was 8:00 a.m., and I was rolling up, to get on with my life. I took my morning constitutional, showered, and shaved. And then I put on prison wear for the last time—blue shirt and jeans. I collected my gear, and then I took the Walkman back to the brother I had borrowed it from. I had about one hour left in here. So I made my rounds to say good-bye to the brothers. At about 9:00 a.m., the loudspeaker called for me and whoever else was leaving this morning to report to Soledad Central,

30

where they would process me out of this godforsaken place.

As I got into the van for the ride to Central, I reflected on all of the times I took this ride for college classes at Central. But this ride was different; I wouldn't be coming back this afternoon. I was outta here. The exit process took about forty-five minutes. I changed from my prison uniform into the jogging suit that my girlfriend Roni had sent me for my civilian dress-outs.

I was traveling in reverse. The way they bring you in is not the same way they take you out—a courtyard that was apparently the common-area quad for the prison administrative offices. I had been here for some time and never imagined any part of the prison looking like this. It was beautiful. There were all of these stones arranged into different designs, laid out in semicircles all over this courtyard, with plants and stuff like that. When I first arrived here and when I returned after being transferred back from San Quentin, what I saw was disgusting. We were brought here in chains like slaves and forced to wait hours in the most horrible of conditions. We were held in this narrow holding area with a toilet that did not work. The toilet was full of feces, so if you had to relieve yourself, it was better to wait until you got to your cell. When I first arrived here from Vacaville, the Northern California CDC receiving center, I had to wait eight hours before being processed.

As I approached the gate, I saw a more beautiful sight: my girlfriend leaning against her car. Man, was she pretty.

A guard hit this release button and I flew through the gate. I was out. I was free at last. Roni had been one of my girl-friends in the Black Panther Party. When I fled and went underground in 1977, I disappeared from her life. When I returned and surrendered in 1980, she was one of the first people to come and visit me. She had left the party and was working as a paralegal in a San Francisco law firm, and during my trial and after my conviction, she was my pri-mary means of support, emotionally and financially.

My first couple of weeks spent on the outside were used to get my legs back under me again, and grounded. It may sound odd, but for one, I had to become familiar with moving objects again, like trucks and cars, buses, trains. I was now able for the first time in years to move physically around without restrictions. The sounds and noises of the outside world were different and now unfamiliar, like birds, airplanes, and such. There is the memory of sounds inside prison that you must shake and get out of your head and system—the sound of the bells or alarms they use to sig-nal lock-ups, chow-hall calls, and almost every other per-tinent prison activity. When you're locked up, you may not see certain things, like a butterfly, or certain birds, or squirrels. You don't see women who are not guards. The opposite goes for female prisoners who don't see men who are not guards or authorities. You miss colors other than blue, green, or gray in my case. On the other hand, visiting day in prison was a break from the viciousness of prison life. It was the only time you were not on guard against the violence in prison, as you knew all of the inmates in the visiting room had been strip search just like you had been. It was a time to enjoy your woman, who was soft and warm and loving in such a hard place. You let your guard down, as it was a lot like being home.

Roni was extremely helpful to me during this early transition period. She supported me financially during that first year or two after prison. Her new friends became my new friends. One in particular was the ex-mother-in-law of Huey P. Newton. And occasionally, we met with other former Panthers. We all drank and smoked, talking about the old days. But these encounters with old comrades were awfully sobering for me. I was more concerned with my future, as their futures had begun. Many had finished school and were moving on with their lives and careers, and it appeared that most were making a smooth transition from the revolution to a normal life. Mine was just beginning.

After a couple of weeks of meeting and hanging out with old friends, I kind of got acclimated to my situation and immediate surroundings. I had been accepted at San Francisco State University. But, as my first semester neared, I really began to feel anxious. I had been used to the classes at Soledad, in a controlled environment, with inmate college students and sympathetic professors. This would be different. I was going to be competing with regular college students and not inmate students who were just programming their prison time in order to get their sentences reduced. (In prison your sentence is reduced by one day for every day you work or attend an education class.)

This was serious. I was now going to be competing in the real world.

I then began to wonder if the professors in prison had cut me some slack, and if my performance was really up to snuff for a regular college program. Nevertheless, I would soon find out.

So in early September, I left my apartment on El Dorado Street in El Cerrito and walked to the local Bay Area Rapid Transit (BART) station. I was extremely nervous, because not only was this the first day of registration at SFSU, but it was the first time I would ride on the BART train. I was riding on new technology, and when the train was elevated, I could look down on the streets I used to run as a member of the Black Panther Party—fast and heavy for almost six years. As I reflected, still alive, about what I had been through, I made a solemn promise to myself that I was going to put 150 percent into everything I did from now on. Because I knew I had to make up for lost time.

I had been out of the normal loop of life for eighteen years. In many ways I felt like I had cheated life with this new start and was concerned that if I now took it for granted, my past would come back to haunt me. After being freed, I reflected a lot on my past, joining the BPP at the tender age of sixteen, rising through the ranks to become assistant chief of staff at the age of twenty-one. I was heavily involved in every aspect of the organization and knew all of the important leaders well. That ended with the firing of a gun. I became a fugitive and eventually a so-called political prisoner. For eighteen years that was all I knew of life as an adult. I felt like the man in Plato's "cave allegory" who was chained inside a cave. After he was released, he ran back into the cave.

While I was a fugitive, I saw the Black Panther Party, the organization that I loved, crumble and dissolve. I now needed to stand on my own two feet and do my own thing. I was still very interested in doing something that would help black people and believed the new path I was forging would do just that.

I did feel, and probably looked, very much out of touch and style. The men looked very confident in their nice business suits as they got off at those BART designations for big business jobs and the like. I also noticed there were probably more women than men, looking all self-assured in their men-like uniforms and smartly tailored dresses. But what probably struck me as being obvious was that every last one of these smartly dressed individuals had worked very hard to get wherever they were going and had been. Most, I assumed, had some kind of education—college, graduate school, etc. If this had been ten years ago, I would have looked at them all as being squares or jug heads going to a (slave) job. I had a renewed respect for them now.

I walked around to survey the campus and to get a feel for my new hangout. There were thousands of people standing in lines at tables registering for classes. Thousands more were sitting on the grass, milling and walking around, and there were also a few groups of students in circles playing hacky sack with their feet. The people on the campus were white, black, brown, Asian, and

Native American; there were adults and young people and many pretty women. This was a real trip for me because I had never in recent years been around this many people who weren't all wearing denim pants and blue shirts. Eventually, I made my way over to the social sciences building to find the office of the professor who would be my advisor. When I arrived, there was a great deal of activity at this location. As I came into the office, I noticed about six or seven white men that I naturally assumed were professors in this department. I introduced myself to one of them, and he said his name was Professor Bailus. This was the man I was looking for. I explained to him where I had taken Professor Brook's class, and to my surprise, he just treated me like I had just walked out of high school or was just another transfer student. As Bailus looked over his copy of my transcript, he noticed that I had taken Brook's Social Sciences Seminar.

"Well," said Bailus, "I know that Robin grades harder than most professors, so what you can do is waive my Senior Seminar, and you will get full credit for Robin's class, and then you can choose another elective course instead."

His words sounded like a vote of confidence. Maybe my prison education was up to standard after all. Maybe I had the right stuff to achieve my goals.

In my first semester I took a couple of classes that would fulfill my General Education requirement for the university system. I then filled out the rest of my course load with a cluster of required social sciences courses. But this first semester was difficult nonetheless, primarily because I had not quite adjusted to being on the outside. In prison I had sat in class with harden criminals who were gaming and killing time while taking classes in the prison college program. Now I was in class with women and men who were all striving to get ahead to get their degrees and move on to become productive people in society. I was also back on the set and was living beyond my luck, so to speak. I knew I was really getting another chance.

I had to make an effort to stay away from Oakland and Richmond. They were my "Red Zones." Or to put it another way, they were high-crime areas where I might run into former inmates from the joint and possibly old friends who were still doing their stuff on the street. I stayed close to home in El Cerrito when I wasn't at the campus. I was making my own way now and needed the space. Not connecting with the old leaders, mentors, and other comrades in the Black Panther Party was a decision I had made as a fugitive. To me that part of my life was over. At least the relationship to a disciplined organization like the Black Panther Party was. I had also met guys in the joint who were real gangsters making big money. They had all said someone like me could go far in the life. I thought better of it because we were all sharing the same prison and that was not cool to me.

By the time the second and final semester rolled around, I was more comfortable. I carried a course load of eighteen units or six classes, including the senior project or senior thesis, but I was more relaxed.

The classes I was taking during this final semester were steering me toward a firm understanding of economics. I was also taking other courses like land-use law and urban studies; urban history; and computer science, where I was learning to write code in Basic for the Apple computers we used. But still, the focus was a core of economics courses like Money and Banking; Computerized Economic Analysis; and a graduate economics seminar titled Applied Micro-Economic Analysis. This last class really stood out because this was some real hard stuff, as the professor kept reminding us. She would say something like this: "Economics is hard, either you get it or you don't." So based on what she said, I had my work cut out for me.

The focus of microeconomics is the individual firm and how it operates in the larger economy. This also included how individuals functioned in the broader or macroeconomic. I was doing a lot of outside reading for this class, and I discovered something that was at first shocking to me, but it also helped me realize that my past experiences would aid me in understanding this real hard stuff. I discovered that there was this correlation between the economic analysis of criminal behavior (assuming you are rational) and how I as an urban guerrilla evaluated risk in some of the operations we conducted in the United States. The more I researched this similarity, the more remarkable it appeared. I guess you can call it intellectual clarity. In fact, the foremost researcher in this space was Gary Becker of the University of Chicago, who would later win a Nobel Prize.

So when it was time for me to select a topic for my final paper in this class, I was pretty sure I had found the perfect topic to write about. But I needed to reflect and think more deeply about what I believed were the real interconnections. We did everything we could in our planning, short of human error, to not get caught on an operation as in most cases we were surely breaking the law. We wore jumpsuits so that if there were any blood splatters, it would not get on our clothing. We wore gloves to conceal fingerprints. (But in my last operation, it did not matter. My hand was shattered, and when I ripped the glove off, the evidence they looked for was someone who had been shot in the right hand.) We used shotguns most of the time because they had smooth bores, which affected most positive ballistics tests. And if a handgun was used, or a weapon with barrel grooves, we just deep-sixed it. There is more, but we did as much as possible to conceal our involvement.

When economists wrote about the rational human being who planned on committing a crime, the discussion sounded very similar to what we tried to do. Or put differently, when you are breaking the law, you try to increase the probability of success as much as you can. For example, the discussion can feature a criminal evaluating success, but then they also can take into account possible failure and the lost income they will forgo if they have to go to prison. Which is important to a criminal when assessing a future crime risk and reward? The latter was going to be the theme for my paper.

I saw an article in the paper about a major art theft that took place at the Louvre in Paris, France. The paintings that were stolen were considered priceless. So this meant that the thieves could not sell the art on the open market and possibly not even on the black market. So for my paper I assumed it was a specialty job planned by an art lover who had unlimited resources. They probably also didn't care who saw this art hanging in their home or were not people who wanted to show off their wealth or art collection. I also assumed that they had a secluded mansion or maybe even an island all to themselves. They would sit in front of this art sipping priceless wine, enjoying this art all by themselves. So most of the assumptions for this applied microeconomic paper were premised on this art lover with unlimited means, who does not have a problem with anonymity.

Now I also assumed this art lover could hire a middleman to front and find the thieves to do this job. Once the thieves have been located and the discussion begins and the art pieces have been identified, that is when the analysis begins. First, if the loot being targeted is considered priceless, the degree of difficulty will enhance the price that the thieves will demand. Also, because the art is priceless, that probably means that if they get caught, the prison time could put them out of business for life. They would probably consider this, but let's assume that they would get twenty years if caught and convicted. So now the thieves are assuming, well, I made this much money this year and it was a good year for stealing stuff. So they assume that if they get caught, they will lose twenty years' worth of that amount. They also assume since the art is priceless that if they get away with the theft they will never be able to work again. So they take this into consideration also, but with compounded interest. So the amount they would charge for the job includes the assumption that if they get caught, they want to get paid, and if they get away, they want to be paid so that they never have to work again.

Now, there is more to this type of project, like building the financial model, setting a discount rate, working with present-value tables, and constructing a cartoon or graph with an X and Y axis to give the professor a visual feel to what you are proposing. I did the work, and the professor called me in to meet with another economics professor one afternoon. The two professors were smiling as they both said great paper, very original, and so how did you come up with this because this is real good work? I told them the truth. I told them that I had been to prison before and that if I were to do a job like this, I would construct a model like this that would yield this kind of decision. My professor just looked at me, smiled again, and wrote an A on the front of my paper.

The work I did on the paper was enlightening because we in the Black Panther Party never thought about money as a factor or calculated what income we would lose if we got caught. Our risk assumptions were a little harsher. In fact, we had three: prison for life, exile for life, or death. However, we did everything we could to avoid capture. The work I did on this paper prepared me intellectually for the next big projects in my life and at school, which were the Senior Project and my new life. I was willing to risk exposure at this point to develop my livelihood, even if it meant some type of failure. I wanted to get ahead and become successful. I was even willing to risk my invisibility and partial anonymity at this early juncture to get ahead. I was trying to become visible and successful at the same time.

I felt I was getting my confidence back. The same confidence I had known back in the day. My work on my senior thesis was nearly complete. The degree I was pursuing, Interdisciplinary Studies in the Social Sciences, was based on the thinking of three seminal figures: Karl Marx, Max Weber, and Sigmund Freud. So my senior thesis had to adopt the theory from at least one these giants. I chose Marxism to analyze the Dow Jones Industrial Average. The assumption is that this daily average or index of thirty large, industrial companies can predict future business conditions going forward for at least six months. This has something to do with statistics and what is called an average, or measuring the central tendency of a group of data. When Charles Dow created the index in the nineteenth century, it was a true average based on the total market value of the thirty companies summed and then divided by thirty. Well, over the years, after stock splits and such, it was no longer a true average. So using a Marxist economic analysis, I was able to show that this index was pretty much a fraud. That is, in its ability to forecast future business conditions. Moreover, Marxism is anticapitalist at its core, so that was the only real conclusion I should have come up with anyway.

More broadly, my senior project began with defining the project, and my statement was: "Is the Dow Jones Industrial Average a true average that is representative of the stock market? As seen through a Marxist methodological stance." There were eleven chapters, with an introduction; a quick Marxist analysis of the stock market; the history of the New York Stock Exchange from 1817 to 1884; the history of the Dow Jones Industrial Average from 1884 to present; the marketplace and the effect on the stock market; the Dow Jones Average–method of computation; a broader look at the other indices, like the New York Stock Exchange and the Standard and Poor's; and then a comparison and contrast of the broader indices and the Dow 30; and the conclusion.

My conclusion read: "I feel most of what has been written will suffice. When I first started this project in the fall of 1985, I was certain I would find that the Dow Jones Industrial Average was not representative of the stock market and did not forecast future business conditions as claimed. I believe that I have proven this, but I also discovered much more. Focusing on the Dow using a methodological stance of Marxism revealed that monopoly controls the entire market. The institutions manipulate the Dow, Standard and Poor 500, and the broader New York Stock Exchange. So in that aspect, the method of computation and sample size is irrelevant. It does not matter how you add up the profits, it still yields the same results: exploitation of workers' labor. It also revealed the perpetration of a slick financial con game. People are led to believe that they have a say in what a company does; that they, along with the institutions, are prospering and all will be well. The fact that should be self-evident to everyone is that business conditions are supposed to control the market. But what I have discovered using a Marxist methodological stance is that the stock market is characteristic of a capitalist system. Capitalists concentrate profits from surplus value in whatever sector of the economy that will yield the best return. Today, they are focusing on the stock market creating profit from the sweat and toil, either physical or intellectual, of exploited workers."

My senior thesis advisor, Professor Miller, had worked with me. It turns out that the subject and approach I chose for my project hadn't been done before. I chose something especially challenging and didn't have a road map for doing it. But I had the support and determination. I worked hard and I got it done. I carried out my plan, taking the big step of graduating. I got an A+ on my senior thesis.

So now the next step, get a job. But within myself, I really began to struggle with a few notions: Was I headed in the right direction academically? And was I really as smart as I thought I was? And how difficult was it going to be to secure a real job, given my felony conviction and prison term?

CHAPTER 5

Work (that Works for You)

"All labor that uplifts humanity has dignity and importance and should be undertaken with painstaking excellence."
—Martin Luther King, Jr.

Every spring, on most college and university campuses, employers recruit. They seek out bright-eyed and freshly scrubbed graduates to hire and renew their depleting ranks. It's something to look forward to and be excited about. I did. I was. But the process was new and foreign. I had never been on a job interview as an adult. The last time I was interviewed for a job, I was a kid in 1966. I hadn't had a paying job since I was a teenager living in San Diego. I was really scared shitless about the recruiting event. I sent my résumé around. In preparation for this venture, I started reading those "how to

get a job" books. I discovered that they were usually written for people making career changes, not starting new
careers or beginning again from scratch in the work world.
The best book for me was *What Color Is Your Parachute?* by
Richard Bolles. I also talked to my parole officer. He was
very cool about the whole thing. He said, "You're better
prepared than most people, so don't worry, you'll do just
fine." *Yeah right*, I thought at the time. But I appreciated
his encouragement.

I blew every interview. How? I fully and honestly dis-
closed that I had been formerly incarcerated. I was really
naive at this point in my journey about my status and
believed the hype about a fair and second chance once I
had served my time. The advice I read in books said that
if you have a felony conviction, you should tell the truth,
up front, during the interview. So I did. And I watched
the interviewers—one after the other—turn colors, drop
pens and pencils, and otherwise come unglued. "I'm sorry,
but, Mr. Forbes, this interview is concluded," they would
say. One got up without a word and just left the office, his
office, and walked out of the building. I just sat there, stu-
pefied. But I remained cool under fire.

But I also began to realize that I was naive in a way
that was surprising, given my background. Me, Buddha
Samurai, Black Panther official, I believe "American
Society and its American Dream" to be forgiving. That this
society valued forgiveness for transgressions against the
judicial system, especially when the offender had redeemed
himself. I thought that someone like me actually had a

right to the fruits of the "American Society" that another man would respect. I had paid my debt to society. The only thing to do now: forge onward.

In early May 1986, it finally came in the mail, approximately two weeks after I had submitted my final documentation notifying the California State University that I had completed my requirements to graduate. A five-by-three-inch manila card bearing an inscription: "Flores Alexander Forbes has fulfilled all of the requirements for his Bachelor of Arts Degree in the Interdisciplinary Studies of the Social Sciences." That was worth all of my previous experience and a very short period of preparation all rolled into one. It said that everything was looking pretty good at this moment in my life. I had practically aced all of my classes, and Professor Miller gave me an A+ on my senior thesis, which was sixty pages long and with a little more work, he said, it could be of publishable quality. I felt like I was "shitin' in tall cotton."

At the same time, I was disturbed. I'm cynical. I questioned whether I could truly make a comeback in life. I pressed on in my job search, in the summer of 1986. Even when you feel discouraged, frustrated, pissed off you have to continue on to make constructive moves. You may not be running yet, but you got to keep walking.

I developed another plan. I sought out this job developer whom a friend had introduced me to. It was more than worth it. The person asked me questions about my life experiences and at the end, helped me write a new and improved résumé.

I rethought the kinds of jobs I was pursuing. I needed to get closer to something that matched my limited academic experience and practically no marketable work experience. I had gone for some marketing and urban planning jobs and that hadn't worked. I also needed to widen my options because I needed immediate cash flow. I would now look for experience-building programs (e.g., internships and fellowships within my field of interest), hopefully attracting a position that I could learn in and gain experience from and also begin to make a living.

I sent my cover letters and new résumés everywhere. I received more rejections than you could shake a stick at, but I also got a few interviews. When the interviewer got to the point in the discussion where they asked: "Is there something else you haven't told us about yourself that we should know?" I replied every single time: "Well, yes, there is, you know, I just got out of prison and . . ." End of discussion. I was really learning the hard way. What I had yet to learn was how to discern how much information to give and to whom. Not every employer requires the same information nor has the same rules. And there are some employers out there who believe in redemption and aren't biased against people who had redeemed themselves. I just had to work harder at finding them.

* * *

"He who opens a school door, closes a prison."
—Victor Hugo

I saw an ad in the paper about Urban Planning at New York University (NYU) and the benefits of studying the field in the city where urban planning actually began in this country. I clipped the ad and sent for a bulletin and application. I applied and was accepted for the next semester, beginning in the fall of 1987.

Without a doubt, the most intriguing thing about going to New York City would be leaving the Bay Area. I felt pain on a daily basis, gazing at my past represented by the same places and faces where the wounds were inflicted. I was recognized here and represented something that garnered respect—was infamous to some, famous to others. My reputation was something that was hip to guys on the street. But to me, inside I wanted to sweep the past—the stuff they admired—under a rug in my new life as a respectable professional with a career in urban planning.

I was proud of the activist part of my past. My work in the movement shaped my self-esteem. My respect for the struggle to liberate black people nourished me. But my understanding of who I was and what I did was deeper, and my consideration of what it meant and means to other people was evolving.

The movement served people in so many ways that the media and politics ignored. We fed people who needed feeding with our breakfast program. We provided health care, giving access to free clinics and other programs. We provided models that have been embraced and copied up to now. But people more often criticized and/or glamorized the role of guns in our work. They liked it when I talked about the stern stuff of politics. I couldn't control the emphasis that people put on the role of guns in my past in the movement. As it related to my image, I believed that many of the negative parts would fade away with time, and my hard work to present myself fully and honestly as I truly am would stand out. More than anything now, though, my personal survival was my focus in this moment in my life. I couldn't get caught up in my past if I really wanted to advance forward.

New York City was a huge move. I was not just leaving my past behind, my reputation, and hopefully that part of me that caused me to take those outrageous chances. I was trying to change, and at this moment, the only way I knew how to change was to move physically from this location that had shaped my life.

But within the happiness and progress of my early reentry success and this next opportunity, my life was changing. Or at least I felt I had to change my life, especially where Roni was involved. I never told her I was not in love with her anymore. Probably because I feared she would walk away and ruin my reentry efforts. This was probably true and explains why I was dishonest with her about my true feelings for some time. I needed her when I was released, and I used her to benefit my selfish need to get ahead. After all, I was the desperate one. I left her long before I actually did, but because of my status as a formerly incarcerated black man, I could not tell her for fear of losing her support. When I told her what my plans were and that they did not include her, she lost it. But she did not kick me out as I thought, but let me walk away when the time was set for me to go.

She has not spoken to me since.

Getting my master's degree was a start. It was important for me to now rebuild my life on paper as a professional. There were practical matters to attend to, but it was also a state of mind. I was feeling like the underdog: outgunned, and outmanned at every turn of the road. I had been rejected at almost every juncture since my release. Now, I was going to do the intelligent thing—get more education, more credentials. I was going to play the game their way and try to be the best at acclimating to this society.

I was broke. I had to take out several thousand dollars in loans for my tuition and fees. The balance of my expenses was defrayed by grants and a work-study job. I registered for four classes, stuff I had not taken before. One afternoon in early September, all of the minority students had been invited to a reception by the school's dean, Alan Altshular. He was a big shot in the field of urban planning in general and in transportation planning in particular. I did a little research and learned that during his graduate school years at the University of Chicago, he did some big things. His research on locating freeways in major urban centers became the paradigm for the field of transportation planning and location analysis for transportation infrastructure. What this meant was that he was the first person to concretely certify that the best policy decision for locating a freeway in most urban areas was to run it through the black community. One reason being that the land is cheaper.

Anyway, I was at this reception at 4 Washington Square North at New York University. There were maybe about twenty or thirty people milling around, professors, students, and other administrators, when I struck up a conversation with Dean Altshular. I felt comfortable with him and shared my complete story. I talked about school and that I wanted to be an urban planner in order to help my people. He talked about different black professionals that he knew and described the various jobs they were doing. He referred to black urban planners who were involved in investment banking and stuff like that. The most prominent black urban planner in the United States according to Altshular was Robert C. Weaver, the first HUD secretary and first black cabinet member in a presidential administration. We soon split off from our conversation and began to mingle, and I started to talk with other faculty members and students. I talked with Diane Lemco. Diane, as I was to learn, was one of the coolest administrators at this school. She seemed to understand a lot about people and was, from what I heard, very instrumental in bringing diversity to the Graduate School for Public Administration's present student body.

The next day, Diane Lemco called me at my apartment, "Hello, Flores, this is Diane Lemco from GPA."

"Hi, how are you doing?" I said.

"Well, Flores, I have great news for you." I didn't respond right away.

"Yeah, okay, what is it?"

"Well, you know you really impressed the dean yesterday at the reception and, well, he wants to award you with a full ride."

Like a fool, I didn't even know what that was. I said, "What's that?"

"It's a fellowship, called a Patricia Roberts Harris Fellowship, and it gives you full tuition and a stipend for the two years it will take you to receive your degree. You should come over here to fill out some papers so that we can make it official." I'm not sure what I said at that point, but I left immediately to collect the first gift I'd gotten in years.

Patricia Harris was an African American lawyer and member of President Johnson's cabinet. It was an honor to receive an acknowledgment in her name. And this was, of course, just what I needed to set my financial situation right so I could do my academic work.

I also met Walter Fields and Earl Simons, two well-dressed and articulate black men who had graduated from historical black colleges and universities. They, like me, were also Harris Fellows. But unlike me, they had not been incarcerated. They had legitimate histories and were able to benefit from that. Walter grew up in New Jersey and Earl was from Brooklyn. They were part of a group of black students I would classify as the new "Talent Tenth." They were well educated and politically astute. We often discussed how we would give back to our people. I loved it, as we were on the same page of life.

Around these brothers I felt comfortable enough to let my guard down. I told them my story. This is how I began to form important relationships and make connections that were meaningful to what I was working to accomplish:

to change my fate and shed the stigma of incarceration. Meeting these two intelligent black men also led me back to my old passion of organizing people. They shared my desire to work on bringing about some structural changes at the university. We began by revitalizing a defunct campus organization called the Black Student Caucus.

There was a severe lack of diversity in the full-time faculty among other problems. This was a major urban-policy school located in the largest urban center in this country and to see no faculty members of color teaching about the urban environment and how to solve those problems didn't seem right to any of us. Dean Altshular had left for Harvard, and he was then replaced by Howard Newman, who, for lack of a better word, was really "cool." Newman had been a major player in the Carter administration as the director of the Health Care Finance Administration at Health and Human Services, and appeared to be concerned with fighting to create more faculty diversity at GPA. So with Dean Newman installed, along with Bob Berne as the vice dean and trusty right-hand man, things started to change. It was this administrative combination, along with Diane Lemco, that helped us make certain significant improvements at this school. Walter, Earl, and I were placed on the Diversity Committee and we began to create and help shape policies that were more relevant to students of color and women. But most importantly, we were instrumental in bringing the only full-time black professor to the program: Walter Stafford.

Professor Stafford was an old civil rights fighter who had belonged to the Student Non-violent Coordinating Committee (SNCC) in the sixties. He had a solid research background in the areas of community economic development and in diversity issues. And he was the first person to point out to me that young black men have no special-interest group to speak on their behalf in this country. (If that is true, then formerly incarcerated black men do not have a special-interest group that reps, or stands up for, them either.) It was his class on community economic development that enlightened me as to the kind of work we were doing in the BPP several years ago. I saw a direct correlation between the community development corporation concept, which established nonprofit development corporations that operated in poor neighborhoods to enhance the quality of life by building affordable housing tied to social services and a more robust comprehensive model, and the Oakland Community Learning Center we established in Oakland, California, which also provided comprehensive education and social services to the community. I had finally found my professional niche.

After digging in and really thinking about this new career path, I started to formulate the idea about what an urban planner was, based on my prior real-world experience.

In my estimation, an urban planner is just a well-trained organizer of people who have a specific interest in how the land gets used, a multifaceted approach that touches on resources, buildings, jobs, and an economic interest.

And this action takes place within some type of regulated political process. So training to be an urban planner involved learning and combining professional disciplines into a gumbo of knowledge, skills, and experiences so that I could communicate and organize a group of people around a plan or initiatives.

So I needed to make sure the training I received at the Wagner School could make a good gumbo of knowledge, skills, and experience. I needed to take classes that enlightened me about the public-policy process and public administration as it related to city/urban planning and the implementation of plans. Since I was going to be in New York City, I needed to understand the history of the New York City Zoning Resolution, the community board process, the Uniformed Land Use Review Procedure, and about the super planner Robert Moses.

I took classes in the areas of finance, economics, and statistics, most notably to get a firm understanding of public finance and how it interacts with the private sector financial intermediaries. And finally, I needed to understand architecture and how to draw and read plans and the broader aspects of the built environment in terms of urban design so that I could communicate effectively with the professionals that made up that space.

* * *

"It always seems impossible until it's done."
—Nelson Mandela

I was on my path to reentry, acclimating into a society that had once labeled me in previous years a revolutionary, outlaw, gunslinger, gunrunner, murderer, fugitive, and convict, and now it would have to refer to me as an urban planner, who was formerly incarcerated.

By the spring of 1989, I felt good about my new life, exercising my body and mind and getting wonderful results. But the thought of graduating was heavy on my mind. I had become comfortable in my present situation, and now I would have to venture again into unchartered waters: finding a real job post–graduate school. I knew I was going to graduate with a 3.25 GPA and some excellent recommendations from my professors and even the school's two deans. I had spoken with Diane Lemco and Irene Rosenswig, the director of Career Development, who was the person that helped you identify your potential job market. I talked to them about how I should handle my prison record on my job search. They told me that the responses to my record would depend upon the specific place and on a case-by-case basis. But, they had friends in different fields at various companies to whom they could refer me to get further information. I even checked with Bruce Richard, an ex-LA Panther who had done prison time, and he referred me to a lawyer who had been in the movement with whom I could talk. She said that state, federal, or city positions required various and different things but commonly did a background check. Private employers were less likely to do extensive background checks and had less access to FBI databases. I gave thought to starting my own company, knowing that this might be the best way to avoid the bias against me.

I was living at Washington Square Village, a graduate student and faculty housing complex in the center of Greenwich Village. Every weekend I would take off from my studies and explore the city just like a tourist. The primary person I hung out with was my roommate Kevin Kiyan, a doctoral candidate in economics. He was from California, and he actually knew my brother Fred Forbes when he was a librarian at UC Irvine during Kevin's undergrad years. We were out every weekend, going to concerts, museums, street fairs, and walking the streets of the city, bar-hopping and just having a ball. Prior to this, I realized, I had lived the life of a monk cloistered in ideology for ten years, a fugitive for three years, and hunkered down in prison for five years, so I really believed I deserved every second of this life as a weekend tourist. But as I walked the streets of the Village, my past was never very far away, especially when we passed Christopher Street.

Back in the day when I was a fugitive, 113 Christopher Street was my safe house. I had been wounded, and after the initial medical care I received in Nevada, I needed another doctor to remove the wires from my bullet-shattered right hand. The underground network brought me to this address where I received further medical treatment, and as a result, I had to convalesce for six months beginning in the fall of 1977. It was spooky, as each time I walked by the location, I just could not believe how my fortunes had changed from a wounded fugitive to an aspiring graduate student about to hit the job market.

On May 19, 1989, I received my Master of Urban Planning degree from the Graduate School for Public Administration, New York University (now the Robert F. Wagner Graduate School for Public Service). I had finally reached my most immediate academic goal and felt certain I was on track with reinventing myself.

And as icing on the cake, I was awarded the Dean's Award for Outstanding Student Leadership. An award I shared with Walter Fields and Earl Simons.

My experience at NYU was humbling and truly uplifting because after I was accepted to the university, this was the first experience since SFSU that I could call objective and where I was evaluated by my ability to compete and not by the skeletons in my walk-in-sized closet. It was humbling in that I did not realize how much I did not know, and it was uplifting to see how freely knowledge was dispensed. All I had to do was show up and be a willing recipient.

One of the lessons I learned at NYU was that it was okay to be different, even if it is radically different from most Americans. I was encouraged to probe, to question, and to discover. On the other hand, I was delusional, as I thought I was being evaluated in this society on what appeared to be a level playing field. I was disarmed to a certain degree and felt totally vulnerable and naive to my real past and current circumstances as a black man in America when I was blindsided one evening after studying in the law school library.

I had finished the research in the library and decided to go back to the Bobst library which was about one long block from Vanderbilt Hall. When I left, it was dark, maybe around 7:00 or 8:00 p.m., and as soon as I got onto the sidewalk, an NYPD patrol car drove up onto the sidewalk to block my path. A cop bolted from the car and asked me to stop. The two cops said that they had received a call and that the caller had identified me as someone who was selling drugs in Washington Square Park. "What?" I said. I was just a little shocked at what they said, and it took me a couple of seconds to get my bearings. But for some reason, the familiarity of this situation made me real comfortable as I challenged their accusations. I said, "I'm a student here at NYU, and I was just coming from this library," pointing back at Vanderbilt, "and I'm now going to that library," pointing in the direction of the Bobst. The two cops looked at each other, and then one of them asked me if they could search my book bag. "No," I said. "Do you have a warrant?" One of the cops said, "Shit, nigger, we don't need a warrant to search your bag. Don't you know the law?" "Yeah," I said, "I do know the law. That's why I asked you for a warrant, because you do need one to search my bag." They were a little startled, and then the other said, "If you go to school here, let's see your ID, and if you don't have one, we are taking you down." I told them I was reaching into my back pocket to get my wallet and produce my ID. I showed it to them, and they said I should be careful out here with such a smart mouth. They got back into their car and pulled off. I stood there for a minute playing with the flashback of these two dumb flatfoots fucking with an innocent man like me who was trying to get his act together. It made me think about the San Diego cops messing with me when I was a kid, and the LAPD and the Oakland Police Department when I was a Panther. *Damn,* I said to myself, *those motherfuckers were easy . . .* and then I blocked the violent thought that crept into my head. Back in the day, this would have been one of those situations that the police would not have reported. I could have been missing in action. *Bad thought Forbes,* I said to myself, *those days are long gone* or at least I wanted those days to be gone. Anyway, I did not know what to do, so I told one of the NYU staff people and asked is there any way I could prevent this and the NYU person said, "I'm sorry to tell you this, Flores, but you are a black man, and they always stop black men in this city like that." The person telling me this was a white woman, and I felt a little stupid after the request. I felt real dumb. But what's a guy to do; after all, I am a black man in America.

CHAPTER 6

Heroes and Ghosts

"The shadow of a mighty Negro past flits through the tale of Ethiopia the shadowy and of the Egypt the Sphinx. Throughout history, the powers of single blacks flash here and there like falling stars, and die sometimes before the world has rightly gauged their brightness.

—W. E. B. Du Bois

"Forbes, did you hear the news?" said my friend Earl when I picked up the phone. He asked without saying hello or anything.

"No, what news?"

He paused for a moment before continuing, "I just heard on the national news that Huey P. Newton was killed in Oakland."

I didn't say a word for a moment. "How did it happen?"

Earl said, "He was shot several times."

"Damn," I said. "Thanks for calling."

I hung up without saying good-bye. I did not feel like crying, nor did I feel a loss at first, because this was Huey. And he was tough. Man was he tough. After a few minutes, I thought about what people say when you hear about a terrible and tragic event that affects you tremendously: Where were you when you heard that Huey P. Newton was dead? At this point, I thought it was very tragic. Because I had heard from certain former Party members that Huey was seriously strung out on drugs and that he had escaped a couple of times from drug-treatment facilities. It never occurred to me that this strong-willed man, this intellectual giant could be broken to the point that this white powder could knock him down. I got more info, and I learned it was a drug deal gone badly, and when I learned more, I wasn't surprised. I remember the Black Guerrilla Family (BGF), a black prison gang in California at Vacaville Prison, telling me upon my arrival that there was a contract on Huey's life. So when I heard that the shooter was a BGF soldier on parole, I said to myself, *This will make that cat a general in the joint.* Damn, Huey, you just had to keep pressuring the scene, pushing everything to the "max," to the edge of the envelope. I heard through the grapevine that Huey was taking these guys' dope from them on the street. He understood that he had his bluff in from the sixties and seventies. It looks like this young brother dared to call that bluff. That was how Huey was and how he probably wanted it to be. Yeah, "true to the game," as he would say.

Huey was really hanging out there, and he was spotted every now and then by someone who used to call him the "Servant of the People," doing things that didn't match that role and reputation. However, the most tragic incident was told to me by this comrade named Johnny Stakes, who says he was floored when it happened. He said he was pulling his car into a liquor store parking lot in Oakland and that a bearded guy approached him and asked for a dollar to buy some beer. Johnny said he told the brother to wait until he got some change and that he would give him the dollar when he finished shopping. Well, Johnny got in the store and thought about how familiar this brother was to him, and when he returned to his car, it hit him like a "sledge hammer." This man was Huey P. Newton.

Sometimes you have to reflect on who your heroes are: the good they do, the harm they do and to whom. But the most important aspect of the crowning of a hero is that you should choose your heroes; even if they are infamous to some and loved by others, it is your choice.

Whether Huey was this tragic figure in American history or not, I believe his contribution to black people in general and to me in particular was enormous. The significance is never lost on me because I went to prison on a charge of felony murder, but the felony that we were committing as previously described was an attempt to kill a witness who was testifying against Huey. However, I grew up and matured after my long ordeal that involved that action. When I turned myself in, I was questioned about Huey's so-called involvement in what became known as the "Richmond Incident." I told them to turn off the tape recorder, read me my rights, and send me to my cell, as I had nothing to say about the charges against me. Even though I never saw Huey again after October 1977, he did leave a message. It was not a letter or note but a human message in the form of a great legal mind that was sent to defend me. That lawyer who knew the law saved my life. So now, Huey and I were even.

He was "larger than life and twice as tall." He was an innovator of the highest degree when he created a vehicle that struck fear into the cowardly police departments of this country that were used to trampling on the rights of black people. He showed genius by creating an organization that displayed manhood and womanhood in the black community as it never had been expressed before and that could stand on its two legs regardless if he were in prison or in exile.

When I think of black men who go to prison, and when they get out, become successful, Huey P. Newton is at the top of the list.

Huey went to prison for killing an Oakland policeman in 1967 and quickly became a cause célèbre with millions of people around the world questioning the charges against him. But when he was freed in 1970, he came back to an organization that he had founded, which had a network with international reach. He soon published three critically reviewed books and continued fantastic organizing feats within the arena of black liberation. Which for all intents and purposes made his short stint in prison a distinguished badge of honor and not the stigma it usually brings. He was a star in some ways, and for the star, the pop-culture icon, serving time can be framed as a badge of honor. Street cred can work in that context, but not in the everyday, workaday world.

Huey educated himself, formally and informally. First, he obtained a doctorate of philosophy from UC Santa Cruz. Second, he created a network of extraordinary forces that included regular folk from the community, politicians, movie stars and other entertainers, noted academics, writers and artists, businesspeople, and the brothers who made up most of the underworld in the San Francisco Oakland Bay Area. Most of this organizing of people took place before he went to prison, and many of them were part of the coalition that worked to free him in 1970. His network, in part, became mine early on in my career in the Black Panther Party.

What he meant to me was something I had never put into words, so hearing of his death was a shock. He had made me realize that I could do almost anything. He had handed me responsibility at a very young age, and that built up my confidence, but what kept ringing in my ear as I tried to drown my growing sorrow with beer was something he used to say: "I want to die young with a pretty body." I don't embrace the idea now, but at one time I did. When I reached my twenty-fifth birthday and was still alive, I felt lucky. I wasn't sure I'd make it. I thought I might die as a Black Panther on some lonely, dark street. I recounted the moments I talked with him during what we called the "mouse trap" period in 1973. A gunman had invaded his home and tried to lay in wait for him and his family to return home to kill him. I was assigned to stand guard in his house to meet the gunman if he returned again. Thank goodness that didn't happen. What did happen is that I got to have long conversations with Huey, staying up all night to talk about life, our struggle, and everything under the sun. That was a great education.

He was a soldier, a leader, but above all, the attribute I most remember and so much wanted to emulate was his intellectual ability and his capacity to share this hunger for knowledge—and with me. I remember how brave he was in the face of danger, and how those moments of impending doom were always framed in a metaphor or simile from some great philosopher's work that he had mastered. It was during these periods of adversity that he could relax a tense group, finger on the trigger and sweat dribbling down your brow, by finding that appropriate quote or phrase and then dressing it up for that exact moment to present in an intense and theatrical soliloquy. He was a brilliant intellectual who brought to the black community manhood, cloaked in academic robes, certifying education's importance on one hand, and on the other, dressed in a black leather jacket and armed with a shotgun and a law book that represented the willingness to defend the principles of our self-determination. He was gone now, and I would never forget him.

* * *

"Guilt is anger directed at ourselves—at what we did or did not do."

—Peter McWilliams

You lose people in the movement. You lose people in the streets. Everybody suffers loss. The relationship between the survivors and the memory and/or ghosts of the movement, the game, the street is particular. This would be brought home to me in some surprising settings, at times I would have never expected, like a book party for Black Panther Elaine Brown at a home on the upper eastside of Manhattan.

I had been at the gathering for about two hours before she, the honored guest, arrived. When she did get there, she was with another former Panther and lifelong friend of mine, Darren Perkins. He was going to travel with her during the upcoming book tour. Elaine Brown had been the chairman of the Black Panther Party from 1974 to 1977 and was also a very dear friend to me. Perkins had been for years a close comrade in the party, as we also worked closely in the underground as members of the party's military arm known as the Buddha Samurai. Perkins looked well-oiled in a glassy-eyed kind of way that was concerning. But I ignored it, tried to mingle and have a good time.

This was a book party, so that was more about wine-splashed conversations about current events and people washing vitamin packets down with expensive wine. These were publishing people who knew each other as agents, writers, editors, publishers. Ken Auletta and his wife, Amanda Urban, were the gracious hosts. I'd read Auletta's work in college, and Amanda is Elaine's literary agent. Author Tony Lukas and I were standing in the hallway having an intense discussion about the race situation in America today. Tony and I had started this conversation the night before at Chin Chin's about the recent "Los Angeles Rebellion." When over the chatter and clanking of beer bottles and wine glasses, I heard a familiar voice shout:

"I'm a disabled, Vietnam combat veteran, and I had over 121 confirmed kills in the bush."

He got louder; everybody else went quiet. My conversation partner Tony Lukas acted like he heard nothing. Perkins was the only person being heard, and he was harsh and clear. I was scared of what was coming next.

I knew it was Perkins, but what I didn't realize was how high or out of control he was getting. He kept on with his diatribe: "I'm a disabled, black, Vietnam combat veteran. I was a member of the Big Red One, attached to the Airborne Rangers. I fought and killed motherfuckers at the Iron Triangle. They had to take away dead muthafuckas in body bags that filled thirty-three Chinook helicopters." This went on and on for about another twenty minutes. This sedate book party had transformed into a chic, Brechtian, black guerrilla theater performance. It was as if Perkins had leapt from the pages of Elaine's memoir, *A Taste of Power*. People may have believed that this was an act being put on in real, live Black Panther style, all for their entertainment. But it was real.

I felt a little nudge against my elbow and turned to see Tony's wife, Linda Healy, Elaine's editor at Random House. She motioned for me to bend over and lend her my ear. I did. "Elaine wants to speak to you, it's urgent."

Her voice was urgent. I excused myself from her husband and followed her through the hall into the plush living room. As we headed toward Elaine, I spied Ken Auletta out of the corner of my eye. He was standing just inside the arch of a doorway, concerned, but maintaining calm.

When I got to Elaine, I could see that she was crying. She grabbed me and kind of scratched at my hand as she pulled me closer. (I hated that, my mother used to do that to me when I was a kid.) Amanda Urban, Linda Healy, and a few other women from Random House were standing protectively around Elaine.

"Flores," said Elaine, "will you help me?"

"Sure," I said, and responded sarcastically, "What's the problem?" We'd known each other too long and too well, not to bring some levity to the situation.

Annoyed with my tone, she said, "It's Perkins, he's gone crazy. He's ruining my book party. Please, Flores, will you talk to him, he'll listen to you, and he respects you. You're the only person here who can control him. Please help me?"

I pulled him aside so we were face to face; "Duke, you are destroying Elaine's moment and scaring all of these people who are just here to celebrate an author. Come on, man, what in the fuck do you think you are doing?"

He said in a pitiful voice, "Fly, I was just trying to help." He cried as I led him to the elevator and down to the street and ushered him into a cab. I later told a teary-eyed Elaine Brown I would accompany her on her book tour instead of Perkins.

Watching Perkins, as Don Freed put it when we visited him in LA, "leap from the pages of Elaine's book," was not a pleasant sight for me. The Duke had been my close friend and comrade for over twenty years, and I did not like seeing him in public like this. Nor did I appreciate him raining on Elaine's parade, or should I say pissing on it with double shots of gin. Perkin's aberrant behavior just confirmed for me how difficult a transformation we as combatants and formerly incarcerated had to make.

*   *   *

"A man should not strive to eliminate his complexes but to get into accord with them: they are legitimately what directs his conduct in the world."

—Sigmund Freud

Even the most together man can have demons, especially when they've been forged in the kinds of fires I have walked in.

I was thirty-seven years old in 1989. I had been a crackerjack Black Panther for ten years; a fugitive for three years; in prison for four years, eight months, and nine days; a college graduate with a social science degree; and now a graduate of an urban-planning graduate school program.

I turned the pages back on my past life in order to get a handle on the present one. But it was difficult and taking a toll on me. I wondered why I made it out when so many of those I had loved and who had struggled alongside me did not. I was not having nightmares and waking up in a cold sweat, but I knew something was affecting me. Call it battle fatigue, post-traumatic stress syndrome, or just being fucked up in the head after living a hard life. I wondered to myself after seeing what happened to Perkins, was that going to happen to me?

Many of my friends, comrades, and loved ones did not make it through the tougher times. And many more were still missing in action. A few, like Geronimo Pratt were still in prison, with very little hope of getting out. (Geronimo's conviction was finally vacated in 1997, and he was released after serving twenty-seven years in prison.) Others, who were involved with the "sterner stuff of politics," like Rollin Reid and Allen "Houseman" Lewis, were lost to the ages, running to beat the "statute of limitations" on their charges. They wandered endlessly from one false ID to another, never able to enjoy life again. I would hear about them and others through the grapevine. I felt fortunate even in my lowest moments, but my thinking was clouded by my sense of loss. And I was in dire need of a job.

By using my contacts at NYU, I was able to avoid any embarrassing moments related to my past while looking and interviewing for a job. I hoped that the degree and the good name of the institution I got it from counted for something.

I landed my first job at a nonprofit community development corporation in Queens, named Woodside on the Move (WOTM). I actually had three offers, and I chose this one because it gave me more responsibility. And, I was pretty sure that they would not do a background check. I was hired as the local economic development specialist for $20,000 a year. That was big bucks for a guy whose last wage was twenty-five cents an hour, working in the furniture shop in the joint. This was my first real job as an adult. I had worked in and for the Black Panther Party. I had gotten my job readiness skills from the party. We were a serious organization and everybody was charged with getting to work on time, working hard, and not causing any friction, just as it would be with any employer.

Anyway, I was the economic development specialist with a staff of two and was responsible for a business development and job development program. Specifically, my job was to manage the commercial revitalization contract that WOTM had with the city's Department of Business Services (DBS). In the beginning, I didn't have a clue what I was supposed to be doing, but I picked things up quickly.

We basically matched unemployed local residents with jobs from a database of about eight hundred to a thousand commercial and manufacturing companies and also provided these applicants with other job placement services. If a local company needed a loan that would create more jobs in the area, via expansion, etc., I functioned as an intermediary between the business and the numerous loan programs that the city offered. I also dealt with financial intermediaries in the private sector, brokering relationships between loan officers and local firms. The primary focus, however, of my contract was to provide assistance via the job development program and promotion services to the major commercial strip on Roosevelt Avenue between 45th Street and 70th Street. For example, I assisted the local merchants with promoting their businesses during holidays. At Christmas time, I raised the money, which came from the local businesses that would benefit, about $17,500, to have lights, decorations, and a mammoth Christmas tree and lighting ceremony in the local square, which was to help draw local residents and the working commuters to the commercial strip for Christmas shopping.

In addition, WOTM was also part of a larger network of CDCs called the Coalition of Neighborhood Economic Development (CNED). This group was organized and staffed by a community development "think tank," the New York Interface Development Project, Inc. (Interface). And from attending these meetings, I could see that this was where the action was. The coalition represented everybody who was somebody in the field of community economic development in NYC. It was clear to me after this introduction that this was the professional network I needed to cultivate going forward. I was intrigued with the Interface staff and their skill at using what was a deftly cultivated network of resources within the city/state public policy apparatus and amongst the private community development world.

The founder and executive director, Stan Litow, was very instrumental in developing the city's education agenda, and shortly after my introduction to this firm, he took most of the staff with him to run New York City's school bureaucracy. As a coalition they designed an agenda that would help get the members of CNED the resources they needed to do their work in the community. For example, they had developed a private/public partnership that provided groups with the soft money they needed for feasibility studies; grants for capital improvements; and in some instances, money for much-needed staff lines. So this public policy advocacy group was very important for the advancement of the local CDC movement by getting them the same access to resources and policy makers that other fledgling industries desired in the city. Most of the groups were multifaceted and were involved in affordable housing development and management; economic development and management of city and state industrial parks and specially designated economic zones; small business development and new business creation; commercial revitalization and job development; and many other community-building activities.

I had always been a fast learner, so it didn't take me long to catch on in my new field. In just two years I was a pretty hot commodity. I was being aggressively courted by this so-called "hush puppy as opposed to white shoe" community development think tank "Interface."

I left Woodside on the Move for Interface without much thought. I had an offer of $32,000 a year on the table. That's a big jump from twenty-five cents an hour and even $20,000 per year. Things were happening fast for me. It was like I was making up for lost time and that was cool. Many times I would wonder how the rest of my old comrades were doing and did they find the going as tough as I had. My right hand with the gunshot wound was completely well now. Most people didn't notice it until they saw the funny way I held a pen or pencil when writing. If anybody asked what had happened to my hand, I told them it was an old baseball injury or some other bullshit.

I kept to myself and to a small group of people that I had met in grad school. I avoided most situations that would bring me into contact with the police or with any situation that would make me respond in a way that would cause people to say, "Hey, how come you seem like you know something about this or that in terms of physical combat, street tactics, etc.?" Later, as I grew bolder, I just didn't care.

Interface turned out to be my window to the big wide world of community development and how the local/state public-policy process was manipulated to further the cause of community building in New York City. On my first day on the job, David Gallagher (DG), my boss, told me to meet him at the office, which was located at 666 Broadway in Greenwich Village. Then from there we would go to Albany, New York, the state capital, to talk to the various legislative committee staff people about Community Economic Development (CED) resources that were being developed and then funneled through the state's premier economic development organization, the Urban Development Corporation (UDC). With our assistance, UDC would in turn offer Requests for Proposals (RFP) designed for CNED member groups. This stuff was definitely cool to me. DG and the previous Interface executives had cultivated some serious connections with key staff members from the Ways and Means Committee, the Speaker's office and a group in the Executive branch called Program and Counsel. The major Interface connection to the governor's office was via UDC, or as DG used to put it, the "Governor's Member Item." So with me in tow, DG would hit the circuit, visiting staff members and discussing the items on his list. This was a major accomplishment for Interface because millions of dollars were becoming available for CDCs that needed resources to conduct studies, develop businesses and business opportunities, infrastructure projects, and other programs that would enhance their ability to do real economic development in their communities.

I was very happy at Interface in the beginning. The money was good, and most of the work involved research, writing, lobbying, and making up new programs for community development groups to take advantage of. It was hard to believe that a person could get paid for this kind of work. It was a snap! It seemed too good to be true. But, internally at Interface, things began to fall apart as foundations and other funders that had supported various programs began to change their guidelines, which affected our funding in specific areas, thus causing us to begin downsizing. So DG, the principal partner at Interface, approached me about leaving and starting our own firm. He said, "I can't do this without you, Flores." So I said, "Let's do it."

DG and I left Interface, and we started the Center for Neighborhood Economic Development, Inc. Now I was making a nice piece of change and getting real comfortable in my field. We were doing the same work with the same clients, just operating under a different corporate name. We now functioned more like consultants, though. We continued the same work with our UDC contracts and maintained our relationships with the foundations that supported the work we were doing with the coalition of CDCs. But we added another piece that was just like hustling on the streets, only without a gun. We began working for fees producing deliverables for different nonprofit clients who needed specific studies done, evaluating the feasibility of going forth with certain projects. Most of these feasibility studies looked at profit-generating enterprises that would move the nonprofit toward self-sufficiency. Simultaneously, I began to be involved in what the Wagner School called the good work of "public service," which I was also getting paid for, too.

Professionally, things were looking pretty good. I was making good money, and the work I was doing fulfilled my appetite for helping my people. But I was bothered by my growing awareness internally of how much more prepared and sophisticated I was than my counterparts who were making more money than me. I felt I should be doing better than I was, relative to my competition. So I turned inward, contemplating on how I could make myself more marketable. I guess this was a good sign for me because in the past the dollar and all that came with it was not very important to me. My value system had been tempered with helping people and not making money and now both were important to me.

I was not really myself, because the person I was projecting to everyone appeared to be ten years younger than I really was. I was basically dissembling and passing on a major scale. In essence, I cut ten years out of my life so that I could fit in without having people who did not know me detect the truth. (These were skills I picked up and perfected as a fugitive.) This was how I handled the issue of the big gap in my work history. I went deep down into myself and said that if I had the courage to do the other things I did in my life, I should be able to muster the courage to come out of the closet and tell my loved ones, new friends, and professional associates that for the last so many years, about six in fact, I have deceived them about who I am and what I've really been in my life.

One by one, I told the whole truth to everyone I needed to, and to my surprise, not one rejected me or got angry. In fact, many people thought it was cool. Among those I told were the brothers I worked with, the people I had gone to school with, and my graduate school roommate.

When you're in the streets like we were back in the day, the truth only matters to the people on your team, especially if you're a fugitive. When you use an alias, it's important to construct a history or a personal story that you can stick to. You must maintain your cover as you move about in your daily life underground. In prison, you hardly ever want to tell the truth, because you don't want those guys getting next to you or your family, and you definitely don't want them to contact you when you hit the streets. I knew there was no real explanation for continuing this charade after I left prison. But when I saw how difficult it was to get a job and make friends, I went all the way in to construct a new history that was true to most people and looked plausible because of the academic credentials I had actually acquired.

In order to come into my true self and move on to the next level in life and work, I had to find a way to live in my truth. So, I had to undo the new fiction that had gotten me to a new and better place, but couldn't take me any further.

I met Calvin Hernton and David Henderson, writers and professors who encouraged me to tell my story in a book. They'd both written classics. Calvin had authored *Sex and Racism in America*. David had written *Jimi Hendrix: Excuse Me While I Kiss the Sky*, a definitive biography of the music legend. They taught at Oberlin and UC Berkeley respectively. Calvin told me that publishing my story would not only document some important history, but reveal myself to many people at one time and separate myself from the crowd. Questions would be answered before they could ask the question.

Opening up and revealing myself to the world so that I could use my entire life experience to inform my performance was one of the best moves in my fledging career I had made to date. And others began to notice, too. I was selected by the Comprehensive Community Revitalization Program to coordinate a joint venture in community building between the Surdna Foundation and six Bronx-based community development corporations. I was positioned at the community development corporation named PROMESA, Inc. This program was part of a funding consortium of fourteen national and corporate foundations as a demonstration project to evaluate the effectiveness of capacity building in distressed neighborhoods. Basically, capacity building meant if you placed skilled and key personnel in a mature community development corporation and gave these people resources and planning/implementation capacity, would this enhance the effort at revitalizing these communities? The entire demonstration was pegged for three years, and then after the planning, resource injection, and other inputs, the six corporations would receive what are called tie-off grants and be on their merry way. The overall budget was around $12,000,000. But through my interaction with this project, I would surmise more money was spent on high-salaried consultants to do the evaluation research and assessment for the funders than on really helping these communities with those dollars. But for me, it was still this fabulous experience that all came about by this lady named Anita Miller. The Comprehensive Community Revitalization Program was her brainchild. Anita was one of the first women program officers at the Ford Foundation and had also worked for Jimmy Carter in his administration as the director of the Federal Home Loan Bank Board. She was considered "Ms. Community Development" in the United States of America.

I remember telling her my story, and in her very gruff manner, she replied, "Good. So you know how to work hard, too." Yes, I did.

Reinvention

"When I found I had crossed that line, I looked at my hands to see if I was the same person. There was such a glory over everything."

　—Harriet Tubman, on her first escape from slavery, 1845

CHAPTER 7

Family

"I'm here because I stand on many, many shoulders, and that's true of every black person I know who has achieved."
—Vernon Jordan

We all have networks, our people, whether it is in a social, religious, or political context. They reflect the order and structure of our lives and are critical to the support system a person needs coming out of confinement and back to visibility. My network as a young boy growing up in Southeast San Diego was broad and robust. I had my family: my parents, Fred and Catherine Forbes; my brother, Fred Jr.; and my younger sister, Katherine. My mother and father were both from North Carolina. My mother was the oldest of thirteen siblings, and my father had five brothers, so I had an enormous extended family that stretched across the United States. And my parents were involved in many civic and faith-based activities in our mostly black community.

Ironically, I was labeled a recalcitrant and expelled from several schools long before reaching high school. I was raised by my father not to take any shit from anyone; that meant students and sometimes even teachers. I would fight at the drop of a hat, usually following an insult to one of my parents. I didn't take playing the dozens well or jokes about my folks. So the label followed me from school to school. Changing schools a lot meant that I got to meet young people from all over San Diego who were black, white, and Chicano. That established my peer network.

I attended Mount Erie Baptist Church, with my mother serving in the youth choir and usher board, and a local Methodist Church that my father attended, which was our faith-based network. Both my parents were very religious. It was par for the course growing up in the South. But during these years, many of my young friends became victims of police repression and their flagrant use of force. On several occasions, my friends and some close partners were the victims of police brutality. And some were even shot to death by the bullets of the San Diego police. It was learned later that during one such incident the victim had a toy gun. I prayed the night following each episode to be saved from a similar fate. One week later after the last incident I, too, was beaten brutally on a football field by a dozen San Diego policemen. I realized that God was not watching over me either, so I dropped Him from my life.

Today, I am still not a religious person, but many are, especially formerly incarcerated guys I know. It's obviously a powerful force—for good and bad. In prison, it's become a way for inmates to seek salvation and for some life and internal improvement inside the joint and when they are released. Many resort to religion in the joint for protection, as many brothers join the Nation of Islam as a shield against the brutality of prison life.

Also in my youth, I played football, baseball, and was even a cub scout and boy scout, interacting with many youth and their adult sponsors throughout San Diego County. All of these early interactions with people became part of my personal network, which would prove lifesaving later in my life in general, but most importantly when I was in prison.

Joining the Black Panther Party at sixteen connected me to a network, a community of people who were extraordinarily dynamic. I was around so many vibrant and smart black people. And to my advantage, most were usually older and more experienced than me, so I listened and learned as much as possible. I was constantly in the presence of the foremost ideologues, teachers, leaders, and the most influential men and women in the BPP. In San Diego, Riverside, Los Angeles, and the San Francisco Oakland Bay Area, I met and interacted with these people who helped me along my way in a very difficult organization to succeed in.

The Black Panther Party was the first real experience I had working within an extremely competitive environment. I wouldn't say that people would literally stab you in the back to get ahead, but one did have to pay close attention, as getting promoted in the Black Panther Party was something everyone sought. So connecting with a strong network in this space was important.

We believed intensely in the old Che Guevara guerrilla warrior adage that "you must develop a face-to-face relationship with your comrades in order to succeed in any undertaking or assignment." We didn't carry business cards to introduce ourselves to each other, but when you did meet someone, that first impression was significant, because the people you met in the Black Panther Party who had influence could help to smooth the way when they saw you were a hard worker. And conversely, if the road to liberation within the organization became difficult as a result of your involvement in some type of disciplinary action these good relationships could help you escape the lash or being mudholed. I worked hard in every assignment, like selling the Black Panther newspaper; organizing and staffing our survival programs, with a specific focus on the Free Breakfast Program for School Children; and when under duress, by showing my courage when the situation got intense involving our enemies. Over the years, I developed a good relationship with people and an even stronger reputation as a hard and selfless worker and a dedicated soldier who took the initiative on all tasks and assignments. It paid off as I began to receive choice assignments and was finally recognized as one of the most trusted members of the rank and file.

One day the minister of education, Raymond "Masai" Hewitt, dropped by my work assignment in San Francisco and told me I had been selected for an elite and special unit that would be involved in what Huey P. Newton called the "sterner stuff of politics." I would learn shortly that this was a euphemism for the violent world of the urban underground. I accepted the assignment, working hard as I continued to work my way up the ranks of the organization. However, one of the most significant aspects of this dangerous work was being involved in the Black Panther Party's underground network. This work included the many machinations of this turbulent environment, involving weapons caches throughout the United States and the always-present covert operation. My involvement in these activities brought me into contact with the many covert operatives that only a few people within the organization knew existed. This work also brought me into contact with the actual underground network of safe houses and the extraordinary forces that facilitated this operation, which was used for operatives like me when we had to flee and avoid capture and/or go into exile. Eventually, my participation in this area of work finally caught up with me in a very personal way. As previously described, I was seriously wounded and my best friend Louis "Texas" Johnson was killed during a botched operation that was staged to kill a witness testifying against Huey P. Newton. As a result, I was to experience a newer and more sophisticated manifestation of this complex network that had become my family.

Historically, when a Panther underground operative was wounded on an operation or incident, we had to rely on outside medical treatment. This meant the person would be arrested soon after they were dropped off at the hospital. But when I was wounded, the organization went out of its way to make sure I was not captured. I was whisked out of state to a hospital in Las Vegas, patched up, and taken across country to Chicago where a group of white sympathizers who called themselves Revolutionary Hillbillies assisted me in my underground journey. My hand had been shattered by a high-velocity bullet, and once it was repaired, I needed further medical assistance with removing the wires that held my hand together. This group took me to their doctor in New York City, where the wires were removed and I began my convalescence on Christopher Street in Greenwich Village, beginning in November 1977. The Young Patriots became my new family for the three years I was a fugitive. I turned myself in on October 23, 1980, and was eventually convicted of felony murder.

When I arrived at Soledad State Prison in 1983, a war over space, drugs, and race had been in progress for at least a decade within the California Department of Corrections. The war was being fought between the various gangs, like the Black Guerrilla Family, the Mexican Mafia, the Aryan Brotherhood, and Nuestra Familia in many of the major prisons like Soledad, San Quentin, Folsom, and Tracey. The prison change movement legend George Jackson, who was a member of the BPP at the time of his death, had some very close ties to the BGF, so as a Panther coming to prison, I heard through the grapevine that they wanted to meet with me. But for anyone coming to the joint in the 1980s in California, the landscape could be treacherous. I remember bumping shoulders physically with this Chicano guy when I was at the Receiving Center in Vacaville, and he commenced to follow me around and was eyeballing me whenever we were in the same quad area. One of the brothers pulled my coat and said he told people he was going to shank me because I disrespected him. I finally confronted him and told him I am not a regular here in the joint and that I am just passing through, so I apologize and now let's drop it. He finally went away, but I realized the space in here was vital and important to a person's self-esteem and made a personal note to stay clear of these idiots in here because that space issue was one of the reasons for the gang war.

Anyway, on my very first day on the yard at Soledad North, I was walking alone around the athletic track when I noticed over a dozen black men eyeballing me. Several walked closer, and as they came near, I stopped. But as I looked over their faces I began to smile. I could hardly contain my astonishment; it was my preteen and teenage network from San Diego. And to my immediate advantage, several of them had become the BGF shot callers on the prison yard. They were childhood friends from Mt. Erie Baptist Church, Alonzo E. Horton Elementary School, and the Southeast Little League and Pony League that I connected with while growing up in San Diego. They were to become my network for survival that would sustain and protect me until I was released in August 1985.

As I began my journey as a formerly incarcerated black man, the network I had stumbled into would show its face early on during my one year on parole. My parole officer told me he used to hang out at the Gardenia Club in Oakland with Huey P. Newton back in the day. The PO told me at my first mandatory interview that you must be a cool brother if that's the company you kept. He told me I am sure you are serious about moving forward with your life, so I will not get in your way. "Call me when your year is up." The day I graduated from college, I called him and he said, "Cool, congrats, you are off parole and good luck."

The track of connections and relationships that made up my network followed me from prison to the streets as the professors at San Francisco State University were tight with the professors who taught in the San José State University prison program at Soledad. That relationship went very well for my transition and the transferring of credits as I matriculated from college in prison to college on the streets. When I landed at NYU for my graduate studies, the administration and faculty were extremely helpful in assisting me with navigating this large urban university as I settled in for a rigorous two years to complete my master's degree in urban planning.

CHAPTER 8

Coworkers and Bosses

"Networks deliver three unique advantages: private information, access to diverse skill sets, and power."
—Brian Uzzi and Shannon Dunlap,
Harvard Business Review

"The last job I applied for was to be a bus driver for the Chicago Transit Authority in 1957."
—Vernon Jordan

W hen I was released from prison in 1985, I moved back to the San Francisco Oakland Bay Area. The Black Panther Party had been defunct since 1982, but several former comrades were organizing a reunion for October 1986, the twentieth anniversary of the party's founding. If this took place, it would be my first reunion of any kind in my life. It did take place, and at the gathering I interacted with my first organized surrounding of what could be called for me a group of coworkers and bosses.

However happy I was to see many of my comrades, I came to a startling realization, and that was, these former coworkers and bosses may not be able to help me in my efforts at reentry. I had to do a quick assessment with this group, something like an evaluation of who could help and who could not help, and the final resolution was that maybe a few could.

Anyone who is on the reentry path must do the same with the associates they were involved with prior to incarceration. The skills and experiences I was taking away from these relationships would be critical to my success going forward, so in many instances, that realization was the only takeaway. I learned to think critically, see the political environment for what it was, and not be fooled by the rhetoric and demagoguery of the politicians. Basically, I learned to see bullshit when it was present. And probably the most important takeaway was the lifelong learning concept I got from the party in the form of reading books to learn.

NYU was a place that socialized a great deal and showing up at one of the many wine sips and other events gave me an opportunity to network with staff, faculty, and fellow students. I realized a major aspect in networking was to make people like you, and get them to be comfortable around you, which in turn would make them hear you when you spoke to them. However, you must remain vigilant when you are a formerly incarcerated black man developing your network and interacting with people who may not know your background yet, so be aware you must be cognizant of what you tell people; it's important. If they are someone you can trust immediately, tell them your story. If you do not trust them, stay in touch so that as you move through life, you can return to them as a colleague and eventually tell them your story. I have met many professionals who have become colleagues, and the moment I told them about my past, they were accepting and very understanding.

I found that once you have begun your journey back, the people who will become your coworkers and bosses really pay attention to you when you're honest about your life. It is not easy, but once you crack the wall here are a few tips. You should keep in mind that they are interested in interacting with you to network, but they also want something from you, too. So exchange cards and information if you have any. Talk about your contacts, especially if it is someone they may want to meet. You cannot believe what people want to hear. After I became comfortable and decided to come out, I used to hold court talking about the BPP. Why? Because it was a complex organization that was very secretive, just as many corporations are. So remember: information is the raw material for new ideas, which people are always looking for. Or put another way, be bold and talk about what you know.

Once you are in the process and are navigating the system that is the world of work, pay attention to the other things that your coworkers and bosses see as vital to advancement. For example, a strong résumé is one item, but make sure you can document your accomplishments, new skills, and takeaway experiences. But also make sure you can always go home again. This means you will always have to get a recommendation from the last place you worked, and you want coworkers and especially bosses to say great things about your work. Other activities in this space also include building on your professional development regardless of your trade or profession. Going to conferences, alumni events, fund-raising galas, and other related activities is also important. And finally within this particular space, one needs to build one's communication skills. If you take any type of class related to communication skill please take a public-speaking course. Not only will it help you in front of a crowd, it will do wonders for you in mingling with a group of prospective people who may want to help you someday. Also check out dressing tips, not just for interviews but for the world of work, as you never want to dress and be out of place. So being in public well dressed and confident helps you with working the room and schmoozing.

During my journey I have applied for fellowships like the Revson Fellowship at Columbia University, which helped me to improve my financial analysis skills by taking classes at the business school and its real estate development program. My references came from former coworkers and bosses who thought I was ideal for this professional development opportunity. But I was more fortunate to socialize with many professional black men in NYC, and when they created this networking group called the Brothers Brunch, I was invited to join. The group was comprised of some of the more successful black men in the field of urban planning, public policy, and public administration. We met on one particular Sunday for about two or three years and had brunch at a restaurant. The relationships I made during this phase have stayed with me until today. In fact, many of the people I work with today while at Columbia University either participated in the brunch or was someone I met indirectly via one of the brothers that participated.

As I moved out of academia into the professional world as an urban planner, my workplace relationships and networking were enormously important, especially given the fact that very few blacks were in the field of urban planning. But a more notable aspect of the professional world of public policy, urban planning, design, and architecture is the fact that many of the people in powerful positions are women. Most of my primary sponsors and supporters in my network are women, who, I am proud to say, are the most enlightened when it comes to giving anyone a second chance.

In fact, just a few years out of graduate school, my prospects were developing very well, so well in fact, from 1997 until today, I never looked for a job, as I was mostly recruited. The opportunities came primarily from women of color, like C. Virginia Fields, who was Manhattan Borough president; Sheena Wright, CEO of Abyssinian

Development Corporation; and Maxine Griffith, executive vice president of Columbia University, who helped me remove the stigma of external incarceration.

A mentor of mine from my Black Panther Party days once told me that everything you need to know about anything can be found in a book somewhere. I have found this wise saying to be true. One of the books we studied in the Black Panther Party was *The Godfather*, by Mario Puzo. Yes, the book was about a criminal organization, but they were also a disciplined organization that ran counter to the legal system at times. The concept of the disciplined organization can give you a unique perspective on the relationship between coworkers and bosses. The most important aspect of this relationship is the building of trust, and trusting each other to do and follow up on tasks. The ability to convey trust beyond just showing up for work on time and doing a good job is the most important lesson a formerly incarcerated person can learn during their journey through reentry. The formerly incarcerated person must build trust with his or her relationships so that once he or she moves on to something more lucrative, the recommendation that is given by a former coworker or boss rings true to the newfound success the person strives for.

CHAPTER 9

Community

"Grant stood by me when I was crazy, and I stood by him when he was drunk, and now we stand by each other."

—William T. Sherman

Historically, the relationship between society and black men in networks, for example, brother to brother in whatever form of grouping or organization, has always been an issue of note within American society. Long before stop-and-frisk and reminiscent of the paddy rollers and slave catchers from antebellum times, it was common knowledge amongst the brothers that if more than three of us were seen congregating or huddling in what appeared to be a conspiratorial manner on a street corner in San Diego, Oakland, or Los Angeles, the police would quickly identify this as a reason to intervene,

99

or swoop, as we refer to it on the street. Sociologist Elijah Anderson's research as reflected in his book *Street Wise* describes it this way: "The downtown police are distant, impersonal and often actively looking for 'trouble.' They are known to swoop down arbitrarily on gatherings of black youth standing on a street corner; they might punch them around, call them names and administer other kinds of abuse, apparently for sport."

Upon my personal reflection and experience, and based on my observation of American society, the only approval of black men getting together, gathering, and developing a network or bonding resource is when eleven black men are huddling on a gridiron or five brothers are huddling to check match-up assignments, before shooting free throws. However, the social terror we have grown up with after years of harassment and police surveillance has been successful in training black men to steer clear of any Nat Turner–type negroes who may have gotten through the roadblocks of conditioning that have made many of us fearful of bonding today in any form. And by "today," I mean here at Columbia University in the city of New York. When I first came to Columbia as an assistant vice president, I began reaching out to other black men on campus who had a similar officer grade, so that we could meet and bond, which is what professionals do in any organization. Moreover, another brother had a similar idea. This brother was a director at Columbia University Facilities, and he told me he was organizing a networking lunch for black men who worked at Columbia in central administration and who had an officer grade of at least thirteen and above.

A few of these lunches were held, and I attended. But nearing the end of one of these lunches, I asked some of the longer-tenured brothers present, is this it with regard to the number of black men at this grade who worked at Columbia? Maybe thirty black men had attended these lunches on a regular basis. Most of them looked at me and smiled, and one of them, a brother who was the human resource person in my department, said no. He said there are about one hundred or more black men at Columbia with a similar grade. The brother who hosted the lunches said he had a good database and had reached out to a broader number of black men than the number that attended. So I asked, why do you think the rest didn't come? The organizer responded, "They're afraid to be seen in a group of other black men at work." "How do you know?" I asked. He said, "I called many of them, and that is what they said."

In my estimation, the concept of networking, socializing, or gathering as black men beyond any acceptable networking community, like a church fellowship, is one that I do not take lightly, especially given how we have been targeted and our movements watched over the years. The federal government plotted to make sure we did not come together, under the auspices of the FBI's Counter Intelligence Program (COINTELPRO) and the proposed vicious scheming that was labeled the King Alfred Plan. John A. Williams has memorialized this plot in his novel

The Man Who Cried I Am, which depicts the tracking of black men and corralling them to be confined in earlier-used concentration camps left vacant by the freeing of Japanese Americans after World War II. Although the Williams depiction is in his classic novel, the King Alfred Plan was to me based on the practice of monitoring black men in America via COINTELPRO, a real CIA scheme to repress and confine people of African descent in America, especially following the rebellions and liberation struggles of the sixties and seventies. Furthermore, the emphasis of these plans was for black people in general, but the specific focus was on black men.

Finally, as black men in America, I think it is important that we all have a clear perspective on our existence as a community. It doesn't matter if you were formerly incarcerated or a professional walking the streets without any restrictions, you are still a black man who has been marked, labeled, and watched. So what I am saying is, we all need each other's help and that help can come in many ways.

All my brothers who can help, just check this out. The minute you go home and take off your Brooks Brothers or Brioni suit and change into a shirt and jeans and get out and about, remember: you look like the rest of us. You could be stopped, and they might beat your ass down. You can say whatever you want, I work here and I went to this school, but what becomes apparent is that like the rest of us, you are marked and targeted and can become a victim, as we are of the same community. So like your brothers that are invisible men, we should all take advantage of the resources to help each other. And we can use your help.

So here are some tips on how you can help your community of invisible men trying to become visible. Most of you go to church. Well, almost all black churches involved in rebuilding their communities have prison ministries, like Abyssinian Baptist Church in Harlem and Riverside Church in Morningside Heights. Also, Union Theological Seminary has a robust reentry program, and all of these services can use you as a mentor. Or maybe you can write a check or do a fund-raiser to attract your colleagues to help.

And if you want to do it another way, there are existing nonprofits and university programs that will surely accept your mentoring assistance, resources, connections, and recognition. Even though my focus is on black men, most of these resources help the formerly incarcerated in general. Like Justleadership, a leadership training program for the formerly incarcerated that was founded by Glenn Martin, one of the major advocates and voices in this space. There is College and Community Fellowship, a program that helps women coming out of prison obtain their higher-education degrees. In addition, there are numerous groups that provide the formerly incarcerated with skills training, life skills, and higher-education opportunities that do require tutors.

And you may be able to help via your alumni network if your school is part of the Consortium for the Liberal Arts in Prison. Some of the members are Bard, Grinnell, and Wesleyan Universities, and Goucher College. And on

a broader scale, Education from the Inside Out is a collaboration of over forty colleges and universities and faith-
based institutions that provide numerous programs for the
formerly incarcerated in general and black men in particular who could use your help.

111th Street Group: A Safe Space

"We meet the third Tuesday of each month from 6:00 p.m. to 8:30 p.m. It is a powerful gathering of the best minds, and we hope you will join us."
—Eddie Ellis, founder of NuLeadership Policy Group for Urban Solutions

I am not sure how other people may feel when they encounter a person or group that shares something unique or exclusive with them, whether the kindred experience is negative or positive. So when I stumbled across a thriving colony of formerly incarcerated professionals while traveling through my professional life, I was surprised and joyful at the same time. Surprised, because in my ignorance about the population of formerly incarcerated people, I never thought about others going through the same trials and challenges I was experiencing; and joyful, for realizing that I was not alone in my plight. At last!

I was invited by a friend to attend a conference at the Schomburg Center for Black Culture in Harlem that was sponsored by the Open Society Institute and had been organized by the NuLeadership Policy Group. NuLeadership had been founded by two black, male, formerly incarcerated professionals, Eddie Ellis and Dr. Divine

Pryor, in order to organize and advocate for the restoration of rights for the formerly incarcerated in the areas of education, employment, and professional certifications. The conference featured several panels all staffed by formerly incarcerated professionals of all races and genders. I was beside myself at the discovery of this colony of people who were just like me. I met Eddie and Divine, and we struck up a professional and friendly relationship that extends until this day. (Sadly, Eddie passed in July 2014.)

Over the next decade, I faithfully collaborated with Eddie and Divine as we talked, schemed, and developed several proposals, mostly envisioning special projects that would provide a broad road map of choices for the formerly incarcerated and that would guarantee the group a collective opportunity at permanently eliminating the possibility of recidivism from their lives. The best comprehensive scheme I believe we came up with was the NuUrban Marshall Plan, as in Thurgood. This plan was designed to create economic development opportunities for the formerly incarcerated in the areas of urban planning, entrepreneurship, small business development, and housing development and construction. (Unfortunately, the plan has yet to come to fruition, but I see it as a work in progress.) But the most fabulous experience and enriching intellectual opportunity that came from this encounter with like-minded fellow travelers arrived in the form of an email in 2012.

The email read, "A Tuesday Discussion group is being convened inviting only formerly incarcerated leaders who are interested in public policy reform. As a group, we will come together monthly to discuss issues of mutual concern, exchange relevant information, determine ways to support each other and propose initiatives upon which we can collaborate." A monthly list of third Tuesday dates followed the invite with a salutation from Eddie Ellis.

The group included Eddie Ellis, who had served twenty-five years and was also a former Panther; Divine Pryor, who had also done at least a decade behind bars and had earned his PhD; Glenn Martin, a vice president at the Fortune Society, a comprehensive reentry group; Vivian Nixon, executive director of College and Community Fellowship, a reentry organization that helped formerly incarcerated women earn higher-education degrees; Mikail DeVeau, another brother who had also served twenty-five years and was working on his PhD while running a reentry group named Citizens Against Recidivism. This organization provided direct services to the formerly incarcerated as well as public recognition and awards to various individuals who were doing great work in the field. Over the years that we met, probably twenty to twenty-five other formerly incarcerated professionals were involved with these discussion groups. Also included was a black woman lawyer named Soffiyah Elijah, executive director of the Correctional Association of New York, who was one of the primary organizers of the group. She hosted the monthly meetings at a law firm she was affiliated with on 111th Street near Malcolm X Boulevard in Harlem. Soffiyah's dedication to our cause has made her an honorary formerly incarcerated professional.

I had not thought of myself as a formerly incarcerated leader but welcomed the invite that would place me in the room with fellow travelers who were struggling to create a forum and a platform that would begin to organize our community as a voice to be heard and listened to. Professionally and intellectually, I would define the 111th Street Group as an informal think tank, but personally, I saw it as this "safe space" or in the clinical sense, as a "group." In conclusion, I was not aware until this interaction of how desperately I had been looking for a forum to share my ideas, concerns, and strategies with other fellow travelers who could possibly help others who shared our similar circumstance.

Regardless of my success in the private sector as a formerly incarcerated black man who had progressed through the system, I was still a novice amongst this group of seasoned veterans. They were part of the reentry industrial complex that was charged to make reentry for those leaving prison a soft and comfortable landing. I was a novice and very curious as a person who wanted to understand the marketplace of ideas that controlled the environment for the formerly incarcerated in America. But what I didn't know or really understand was that I was in the room because they thought I knew the secret to reentry as expressed by my life's journey and my experience working through the intricacies of the public and private sectors. This belief was brought to my attention when several of them pointed out to me that the majority of educated and trained formerly incarcerated professionals worked in the reentry industry, social services, and programs that provided direct services to the formerly incarcerated. Nevertheless, I listened and learned a great deal.

The complexity and understanding of their relationships within this marketplace of ideas reared its shrewd head from the beginning. The group began by developing criteria for who should be invited and included in the group. First, you had to be formerly incarcerated; second, someone from the original group had to invite you to the meeting, but initially, only as a guest to be scrutinized; and third, you had to be nondisruptive and respectful of all in the group. It didn't take me long to realize that there were folks they didn't want in the room.

Over the next eighteen months, we covered a plethora of issues, all exceedingly important to formerly incarcerated people across the country. In low-key discussions that often became heated, we debated the development of stakeholder interest and how to create a recognizable synergy that would encompass the voices of the formerly incarcerated around the country. How could we concentrate this energy and ability to better inform, represent, and advocate for the formerly incarcerated? These conversations led to a thought process that strategized about the creation of a special-interest group that would assist all who wanted to "come out" and work toward removing the stigma of incarceration from their lives.

I attended these meetings dutifully, as it became clearer and clearer as time went by that the 111th Street Group represented a form of group therapy for me. After a while I began to speak up and reveal my life to those who did not know my story. I told the group how they were helping me to take control of my reality and how they were helping me to defeat the still-present notions of avoidance and isolation which I harbored internally and feared one day would eliminate me as a person. The understanding of the psychic damage post-incarceration can cause was strong within this group; I think we all began to feed on that vibe. More importantly, I was gaining a better understanding of the new language they had been working on in their separate lives which would define the formerly incarcerated in our terms and how we wanted to be seen by the outside world. The most powerful and accepted change came to this language from Eddie Ellis, who is given most of the credit for coining the term "formerly incarcerated" to compete against the arcane and negative expressions that many people use: "ex-con" or "ex-convict."

Their desire to create and bring about fundamental change in the criminal justice system by organizing and developing a lobbying front that would protect the formerly incarcerated from being destroyed convinced me that whatever I did next I had to give back and help the cause by any means necessary. But to my surprise, I had already done my part. I got a phone call one day at work from Mikail DeVeau, the cofounder of Citizens Against Recidivism, Inc., the advocacy and direct social service provider that held an annual awards ceremony celebrating the work of the formerly incarcerated professional. Mikail said that he had placed my name into nomination for the Eddie Ellis Lifetime Achievement Award and that his board had approved the bestowment of the honor. Who would have thought that staying out of prison for more than twenty-five years would garner such an important recognition from my peers?

CHAPTER 10

Mental and Physical Health

"Success is to be measured not so much by the position that one has reached in life as by the obstacles which he has overcome."

—Booker T. Washington

Sometimes I feel like a walking and breathing marked man, with a target on my back or on my forehead. I often wonder if other black men in America feel the same way. I remember my mother saying to me, "Boy, be careful, I wouldn't want you to get lynched." I wonder how many other black men in the 1960s heard this from their mothers. (I did, however, get my ass kidnapped and beaten by the police during these periods of admonition.) I grew up with a stigma attached to my life. Early on I realized as a black man in America if I didn't think in these negative but conscious terms, it could be fatal, like three strikes and you are out.

The first strike I was acutely aware of was just being who I am: a black man in America. The second strike was having lived a difficult, or put more plainly, a shady life. On the other hand, the second strike for me is somewhat more ambivalent than most black men in America have to face and sometimes it's viewed as positive. I was in the Black Panther Party for ten years. That's a major positive in the African American community and in certain parts of America. It's also positive in most areas where mother country radicals reside and amongst intellectuals who don't smoke pipes and wear tweed jackets with patches on their elbows. The ones that smoke pipes and wear corduroy jackets today are trying to say I am a converted terrorist. I actually get cool points (something like street credibility) in my professional life because even though I can't put it on my résumé, it counts as good, solid experience with most intelligent human beings. Being a fugitive is just too vague. People can't really relate to disappearing acts unless you can confirm that you were in the wilderness, meditating on the top of a mountain, chanting and holding hands with a little fat man, or something similar. They say stuff like, well, you must have been guilty. But the biggest strike against me is my two major felony convictions. The first in 1974 was for assaulting an Oakland policeman who was attacking Huey P. Newton. This occurred during a joint arrest by the US Treasury Department's Alcohol, Tobacco, and Firearms Division in collaboration with the Oakland

Police Department in a nightclub, and the second was for felony murder with an arming and use clause. The last conviction is aggravated by the fact that I went to prison most ostensibly as a black man who used a gun aggressively in America. This is the stigma I had to overcome.

In the mid-1990s, the direction my life took began to expose me to a vast new frontier of electrifying and invigorating possibilities that would aid me in removing the stigma of being formerly incarcerated as a black man living in America. Professionally, I was peaking, but I hit a snag at what I thought was my dream job, but ironically, this kerfuffle brought about a great transition that helped me in my life's journey.

I got fired, and it was the best thing that happened to me in 1996. The leadership at PROMESA, a community development corporation in the Bronx, New York, changed from CEO Felix Velasquez, the guy who hired me, to a new CEO, Ruben Medina. After this change, he promptly told me that he could do my job in addition to his and as a result he was eliminating my position. At first I was stunned, since I hadn't been in the workforce that long anyway, so I hadn't experienced this abrupt cash-flow cut off before and what it can do to you psychologically. But the shock and immediacy went away as another prospect quickly opened up a new opportunity for me: writing.

I did not realize it in the beginning, but writing about myself would help me think through my life journey. And it would expose me to a type of intellectual reflection that would prove invaluable for me professionally, politically, socially, and mentally. I wrote my story in the raw, telling my tale from an early age in San Diego, joining the BPP, getting shot, becoming a fugitive, and going to prison. Putting the words to paper about my life journey was soothing to my soul. Most of what I wrote became the foundation for my memoir that was published in 2006. And as my professional life continued to progress, I began to think more seriously about my future beyond just working as an urban planner and was developing a more strategic perspective that would free me of my stigma. On the other hand, at this instance I did not refer to it as a stigma but just surviving in America, and being stuck in my new life.

However, in 1999, two significant events took place that would signal my overcoming the stigma externally and internally. I had been recruited by the New York County executive as a city planner that would spearhead borough president C. Virginia Fields's major revitalization effort in Harlem. She wanted to revitalize and restore sixteen acres of vacant land along Frederick Douglass Boulevard, beginning at 110th Street and ending at 135th Street. My friend from graduate school Earl Simons was the director of the Manhattan Borough President's Northern Manhattan Office, and he had convinced me to take the position and do this very important urban planning work in the Village of Harlem. On the other hand, the most noteworthy aspect of this request was Earl's assurance that by telling the truth during the background check, my getting the job was guaranteed. Earl knew about my past prison term and felony convictions, as did C. Virginia Fields and her general counsel, Denise Outram.

It had been fourteen or fifteen years since my release from prison, and I was ten years out of graduate school. So as an urban planner I had about eleven years of work experience. A stint in the public sector was extremely important for my career trajectory. Based on an assessment of the urban planning field, in order for a professional urban planner to acquire adequate professional experience, at some point during their career they need to serve in a policy-making position in a city, state, federal, or county planning function. The position as the deputy director for land use, planning, and development in the Borough of Manhattan in New York City would more than complete that requirement.

I definitely accepted the job and about two months into the work at the Manhattan Borough President's Office, I was called by the Department of Investigation and told to report to their offices to begin the background check process. I had to fill out several long forms and provide other attachments related to my credit background, past addresses, city, state, and federal taxes, and provide at my expense two sets of fingerprints: one for New York State and the second for the Federal Bureau of Investigation (FBI). Regardless of the borough president's assurances, I cringed through the entire ordeal. But something told me to trust C. Virginia Fields. She was a real soldier, who had marched with Dr. King in Alabama, and as a social worker, she ran an alternative to incarceration program in Brooklyn. She also personally told me that I deserved this second chance in life. Moreover, as I kept reminding myself, this was really more about survival and advancement, and I needed to take the risk to stay on track and to move forward with my life.

As I reflected, taking chances at this point in my life was not new. The experience of risk behavior was a skill I had picked up in the Black Panther Party, and it was pretty much ingrained, and I appreciated the fact that I could gauge the risk when trying to overcome the current obstacles in my life. However, I had not realized until graduate school that one's risk behavior could be measured as a probability exercise, which was very cool.

Anyway, on July 16, 1999, I received a phone call from the New York City Department of Investigation, and the case officer began the conversation like this. He first said all pertinent information was confirmed, like my education, credit review, and that the results for my fingerprints had been logged in. Obviously, there was nothing to report from New York State, but that the FBI query was another issue. Continuing, he said I had eight major felony arrests, two felony convictions, and a four-year, nine-month state prison term. He asked, "What in the hell were you doing?" I said, "I was in the Black Panther Party for ten years." He responded with a slight chuckle and said, "Oh, I see, I understand. Now let's discuss your taxes." I felt physically numb for the balance of the day. It was a weird feeling to be, for lack of a better word, felony-free. I had been persistent and focused. And with a lot of luck, education, a solid network of professional and personal support, I had removed the stigma from my life. I was now breathing cleaner air as a black man that had been to prison and was now living without the external stigma of incarceration and was successful in America. I could literally get on with my life and not carry the stain, humiliation, and human baggage of being formerly incarcerated. The first person I had to tell was the very person who was helping me to remove the mental or internal stigma from my existence: my psychologist Dr. Wilkes.

I had started seeing Dr. Quinton Wilkes in 1999 at the insistence of my woman, Jill Nelson, who thought I had this crazy look or mask on my face that came from my eighteen years of toil in the revolution and prison. According to her, it's a look that makes people say, "Why are you looking at me like that?" And you have no idea what they mean. So seeing a psychologist was a major breakthrough for me because I believed, given my past lifestyle, I would never be able to confide in anyone because I had too many secrets to conceal. I was also arrogant enough to believe that no mental health professional could understand where I had been in life, let alone being able to ever help me. I was a black man in America, and we didn't talk to shrinks because that was an admission of defeat in this country. But Dr. Wilkes was different. He looked like Frederick Douglass and he also knew something about my life choice, primarily the BPP saga. Dr. Wilkes, who was the founder of the African American Studies Program at Fordham University, told me he had treated several former

Panthers at his substance abuse practice in New Jersey. So once I revealed that aspect of my life to him, I thought we really clicked as doctor and patient. Because of that and his confidentiality I told him everything.

Most of the time he just listened and nodded his head, but when I started to open up about the "sterner stuff of politics," and being a fugitive and life in prison, well, he started asking me questions. How did you absolve the thin line between breaking the law and performing a revolutionary act? How did this make you feel, especially when you harmed people? And the questions went on and on. I responded as honestly as I could because I had never been asked questions about any of this stuff. Several times during these sessions, I asked him questions like, "How solid is the confidentiality between me and you?" He responded the same way every time, "Very solid."

I saw Dr. Wilkes from 1999 to 2001 and after a few sessions I realized I needed this deep reflection and open introspection with a mental health professional for one hour a week to help free my tormented soul. I was truly struggling mentally with the transition in my life. I was a survivor of the revolution. I was also a black man in a serious policy-making position in New York City government. And as it were, there weren't many black men present in this environment, so most of the time when I was in a meeting, I was the only black man present. In addition, this was compounded by life's day-to-day grind of being formerly incarcerated, so these sessions became an important part of my life journey.

While I was in prison, my mental health focus was keenly channeled toward my physical well-being. I made sure to organize my brain and how I dealt with the harsh world of prison by staying alert mentally and thereby staying alive. Physical survival was the most important goal in prison. But the discussion of or interest in mental health in prison was usually related to someone trying to avoid their daily programming by faking a mental moment so that they could get sent to the psych ward. And some guys faked mental disorders so that they could get on medication. But there were also numerous light and comedic moments connected to an inmate's mental health.

There was this one brother from the Bay Area who used to pull this stunt on a weekly basis in the chow hall at Soledad State Prison. It was obvious that the guards knew something about his antics because they never took steps to detain him when he acted out. It just scared the shit out of the newer inmates. This brother used to walk into the chow hall and get in line. And as the line moved along, he would step out of the line and shout at the top of his voice: "DON'T MAKE ME KILL AGAIN." The chow hall would become silent and the newer inmates would look around nervously. This brother would then break out into this hysterical laughter and then get silent. He would then get back into line and wait to be served. He was not crazy, but funny, in a place where there weren't many laughs during the course of a day.

As I mentioned earlier, while in prison one's physical well-being was very important. I prepared myself, as did most inmates, by working out vigorously. I had a cell work-out routine, which consisted of fifty push-ups and the same number of sit-ups. Every other day I did deep knee bends. I worked out on the weight pile four times a week with my workout group. On the weight pile everyone worked out with a group for security reasons. This was done because most of the altercations and stabbings took place in the weight pile. And almost all of the weight lifting groups were segregated by race, gang affiliation, or just one's reg-ular workout partners.

Today, I still work out five times week, employing the same prison rigor.

Dr. Wilkes's couch and his office (there were couches on three walls and a big chair on one wall, where he sat) was a safe space where I could talk about my past and my dreams. And I could also talk about how life affected me contemporarily and how I feared the real or pre-sumed pressure as a black man doing well in America. Professionally, I was moving through some significant career moves while I was seeing Dr. Wilkes. I was able to bounce many of these concerns off him on a weekly basis. I could talk to him about my colleagues at the Manhattan Borough President's Office and strategize about how to maneuver and overcome the roadblocks they created within this bureaucratic system. Oftentimes I just needed him to help me come to the self-realization that many of my colleagues that were fronting a strong professional game were not that smart. So with his clinical help in exor-cising my past and the extra reading I was doing on mental health issues, I started to see how this mental health fitness paid off. He was, above all, a great listener.

But around 2001, as I continued to pour my heart and soul out to this man, I started to see from my session notes I was repeating myself and going over the same life material session after session. When I was outside of his office, I felt much more confident and could see a pathway into my future without a personal boogeyman. I had stopped having this one dream that placed me in a chair as I was questioned by some faceless person. It was like this interview scenario and as each question was put to me, I stuttered and began sweating profusely. It reminded me of the sitcom *Sanford and Son* when Fred's friend Grady is on the witness stand testifying against this threatening drug dealer. Grady starts to sweat, with water overflowing from his natural hairstyle, as he stumbles over his answer in fear for his life. That was a recurring dream that went away one night and never came back.

But I didn't realize I should stop seeing my psychologist until I went to Dr. Wilkes's office at the time of my allotted appointment and he told me he had changed the schedule and that I should come back. Immediately, I understood that this was a sign that I should end the counseling. I told him thanks and that I would not need his services anymore. I handed him a check, thanking him heartily with a bro hug and left. I did call him the next day and explained that all good things must come to an end and the reason I stopped seeing him in a blink was I realized I had gone as far as I could and graciously explained to him I think I can make it on my own from here on out. The debriefing that I had so desperately needed years ago was over as I felt so much like a black man living in America who possibly had a chance in the future, stigma-free.

But then again, the psychological work and understanding that I had just been through with Dr. Wilkes did not end with my ending the sessions. I remained curious about what Claude Steele describes in his book *Whistling Vivaldi* as "identity contingencies—the things you have to deal with in a situation because you have a given social identity, because you are old, young, gay, a white male, a woman, black, Latino, politically conservative or liberal, diagnosed with bipolar disorder, a cancer patient and so on." And I will add: a black man who was formerly incarcerated.

My boogeyman was dead.

The Frederick Douglass Boulevard Initiative: City/Urban Planning

"Enforced residential segregation, the most stubborn and universal of the Negro's disadvantages, often leads to exploitation and effects a spatial pattern which facilitates neglect of public services in the well-defined areas where Negroes live. It restricts the opportunities of the more successful as well as the least successful in the group, augmenting artificially the number of non-whites who live in areas of blight and neglect and face impediments to the attainment of values and behavior required for upward social and economic mobility."

—Robert C. Weaver, first United States Housing and Urban Development secretary and the first black member of a presidential cabinet

I first met Robert C. Weaver while I was a graduate student at the Wagner School, New York University. He inspired me to focus on helping black people as an urban planner, because we needed help from people like him who fought the good fight against great odds. His comments above speak to that fight against other urban planners who did not look like us and who did not include us in their urban-planning constructs. Frederick Douglass Boulevard

125

in Harlem was one such victim of this neglectful planning, which at the time was labeled "Urban Renewal." Black people called it "Negro Removal."

When I said I wanted to be an urban planner so that I could help black people in particular and other populations in general, I was serious. But now that I was free to really practice, having removed the stigma of incarceration, I was raring to get my feet wet. I was feeling pretty whole. No ghosts, no boogeymen, no tail of the stigma following me around, and no concerns about the life I had led. I was operating on all cylinders as the playing field for me was finally level.

The project I was hired to focus on at the Manhattan Borough President's Office was introduced to me by a story that C. Virginia Fields told. Virginia lived in Harlem and her driver used to travel down Frederick Douglass Boulevard as she headed to her office in Lower Manhattan. She told me it was disturbing to ride down that street every day and see the vacant land and the blight. She asked herself, *How can I use my office to change that horrible landscape?*

Now I had been hired as the deputy director of land use in her office which involved a broader portfolio than just the soon-to-be-named Frederick Douglass Boulevard Initiative. The City of New York had a complex land-use process that was called the Uniform Land Use Review Procedure or ULURP. Based on a voluminous New York City Zoning Resolution, if a developer wanted to do a project that was not neatly defined in this book of several hundred pages, they could go through a process to change the project, like enhancing the zoning so that they could add more square footage. The process to make these changes involved this public approval process called ULURP. The process began with an application by a developer to the New York City Department of City Planning. Once this application was certified, what was called the ULURP clock would begin. The application would be reviewed by the local Community Board, the Borough president's office, the City Planning Commission, and the New York City Council. And if approved the mayor would sign off and the changes would become part of the developer's project. I was part of the process that involved the Borough president's office.

The Frederick Douglass Boulevard Initiative was my primary focus at the Manhattan Borough President's Office with regard to land use, planning, and development. And from what I could glean from other research I was doing to prepare for the project, it was one of the first efforts like it to take place in Harlem. There had been other planning efforts in Harlem, mostly bringing back, with new construction or gut rehabilitation, a sizable portion of affordable housing. But what Virginia wanted to do was to plan and develop these sixteen acres of vacant land as a mixed-income planned area. Most of the vacant land in this area had been vacant for over twenty-five years; it was cleared as part of the Urban Renewal Plan under Robert Moses, the super planner from the late forties to the late sixties. But as mentioned previously, black people called that planning process "Negro Removal."

One of the first things I had to do was connect with the consultant that Virginia wanted to do the urban design plan for the project. The consultant was an urban planning professor from Columbia University named Lionel McIntyre, who was really an old-school radical. The name of his technical assistance group at the university was the Urban Technical Assistance Project. Lionel was a former member of the Student Non-Violent Coordinating Committee and a serious Marxist urban planner. His shop, the Urban Technical Assistance Project, was commissioned by the Manhattan Borough President's Office to do the base studies for the breadth of the project from 110th Street to 135th Street along Frederick Douglass Boulevard. Mac, as we all called him, was really tight with one of my former graduate school professors, Walter Stafford.

Working with Mac and his team, we began researching and developing the documents that would provide us with a baseline of data so we could move forward with the project. The plan would look at the existing conditions for the project area and then make recommendations on the assumptions of the number of units possible and the square footage that would be available for commercial and community facility use. So we looked at height, set back, and bulk and façade type, and materials for the proposed new buildings. We developed design guidelines that would comport to new zoning-change proposals and identified streetscape improvements. Two major monuments were also proposed: one a traffic-calming structure at 110th Street and Frederick Douglass Boulevard, which would include a statue of the abolitionist Frederick Douglass; and another at a square on 122nd Street, which would have a statue of Underground Railroad conductor Harriet Tubman.

Once the baseline data and studies were compiled, we set out to develop the implementation plan with this abolitionist theme. Because this was a complex urban-planning project that was basically a public, private, and civic collaboration, we decided to phase the project in, working via the city's project-management process. We began to circulate the study and do outreach to the agencies we had to work with in order to get this done. For example, the land use and zoning changes would involve the New York City Department of City Planning. The housing process would involve the city's Housing Preservation and Development agency. The monuments and streetscaping components would become projects with the New York City Department of Transportation and the Economic Development Corporation. In addition, we would have to work with the Department of Cultural Affairs specifically on the monuments. And because we were using funding from the United States Department of Transportation, a member item from Congressman Rangel's office, we had to also work with the New York State Empire Development Corporation, which was the state intermediary for the federal funding.

I was awash in the United States government public-policy apparatus, which was an experience I could have never envisioned as a formerly incarcerated black man navigating the system. But here I was, and I loved it. Moreover, this was a cool experience with Lionel, as he was a staunch Marxist urban planner, kicking and screaming because this was some serious red tape and time-consuming stuff.

I mapped out a detailed schedule, and we got to work. First, we engaged the Department of City Planning to start the zoning change process, as we both thought this would take the most time. Our liaison at City Planning was this cool brother named Edwin Marshall. He explained that we had two tracks that we could move this project through. The first and the most cumbersome was if we had to go through the Uniform Land Use Review Procedure, which would also involve the painstaking creation of an Environmental Impact Statement. This would take two years. The second, and the route we desired, was to shorten the process and have a favorable in-house determination by City Planning, so we would conduct an Environmental Assessment Statement, which would take about six months. The determination was favorable, so we did the latter.

Once that was in order, we began the engagement process for the other city and state partners needed to implement the project. Another aspect that was very complex was the planning, development, and sourcing for the two monuments. This process would involve more not just collaboration, but money. The Borough president was very generous with her capital budget with regard to seeding these projects. And it also helped that my friend Earl Simons was deeply involved as the director of the Borough President's Northern Manhattan Office in addition to Virginia's very capable budget director, Georgianna Streeter. Virginia committed almost $4 million to the Tubman Memorial and landscaping for the triangle location of 122nd and Frederick Douglass Boulevard and $1 million to the Frederick Douglass Circle statue and landscaping for the traffic-calming square at the intersection of 110th Street and Frederick Douglass Boulevard.

Now, once the resources were in place, we began the project planning for these anchor and themed monuments so that they could become real and active projects within the city's project-management process. This meant that for each project that was funded, the specific city agency charged with that function would assign senior staff, like assistant commissioners and project-management staff, to implement the project and bring it to fruition. We also had to organize other local stakeholders, like the arts and architectural historians, around these projects. Two agencies in particular were key with an endeavor like this: the Department of Cultural Affairs and the Department of Transportation.

With the collaboration of these agencies and local stakeholders, like architectural historian John Reddick, we set out to identify artists who could design the monuments. This involved a Request for Expression of Interest that was sent out to artists in this country and beyond. We got responses from some of the most famous artists in the world, like Elizabeth Catlett, Kara Walker, and others. We held planning charrettes to plan out what the sites should look like and finally selected the artist to design both monuments.

I actually thought things were moving along smoothly, until we had to make the biggest lift of all and that was getting the mayor's office to cooperate on getting the city-owned land and placing it in a Request for Proposal process that would engage the New York City Department of Housing Preservation and Development. The problem was that Mayor Rudolph Giuliani had made a pronouncement that he was not talking to nor working with black elected officials in New York City. Virginia was one of the black politicians on his list.

Virginia was a black woman working in a space that was filled with mostly black men with regard to politics in Harlem, but she had a sure trump card in this respect. She was a member in very good standing of the Abyssinian Baptist Church and very close to the church's senior pastor, Reverend Calvin O. Butts. But more importantly, another member of that church was the commissioner of the Department of Housing Preservation and Development, Richard Roberts.

When the team took this problem to Virginia, it did not take long for a grand meeting to get on the calendar to discuss the process for disposition of the sixteen acres along Frederick Douglass Boulevard that were in question. Richard showed up with his team and Virginia showed up with hers, and after a few weeks of back and forth, follow-up discussions, we had a deal.

Everything was tight and coming together, so the last step in the phasing plan was organizing two marketing conferences to bring the developers and the community together with the public sector to make it happen. I had gained experience in the Black Panther Party and at Interface in organizing large conferences, so I set up shop and began the last climb. I began by compiling a list of all of the developers in New York City, large private guys, who did mostly union deals, and even the affordable-housing sector, who developed most nonunion projects. I sought out financial intermediaries, architects, and local community development corporations, as well as national intermediaries, like the Enterprise Foundation and the Local Initiative Support Corporation. We held the conferences at the Adam Clayton Powell State Office Building in Harlem. We rented buses, loaded the developers into the buses, and took them on a tour of the project sites.

Today, in 2016, this project has come to fruition with at least sixteen hundred units of mixed-income housing and a flourishing restaurant row. It is all anchored to the south by the Frederick Douglass Circle statue and memorial and on the north, by the Harriet Tubman Triangle and statue.

I often wonder: Is there anybody who thinks twice about hiring me just because I checked yes on the Box? I am sure there are others who check yes on the Box who can do just as good of a job as I can.

CHAPTER 11

Becoming Visible Men

"Growing numbers of blacks are openly passed over when paroles are considered. They have become aware that their only hope lies in resistance. They have learned that resistance is actually possible. The holds are beginning to slip away. Very few men imprisoned for economic crimes or even crimes of passion against the oppressor feel that they are really guilty."

—George Jackson, Soledad Brother

When I ponder the question about what groups and ideas really influenced the creation of the prison change movement during the 1960s and 1970s in California, what comes to mind are the ideologies and philosophies of the Black Power / Black Liberation Movement. The prison change movement was in my estimation the beginning of an effort by the invisible men in prison to make themselves visible to the public as they fought for their humanity behind bars. This movement reached its apex when the spine-chilling death screams that emanated from the San Quentin Adjustment Center one summer afternoon in 1971 aroused the California Department of Corrections to just how serious the situation had become. The invisible men, led by George Jackson, who were shuttered away and often tortured, were fighting back to the death.

They were demanding to be seen.

What intrigued me about San Quentin was the deep connection to my past. As I was being led across the courtyard one day not long after my arrival, I felt this numbing sensation in my legs. But I kept walking because my mind was racing with the knowledge that George Jackson was killed while trying to gain his freedom through these very same gates and in this courtyard. I could feel the difference in this place as opposed to any other prison. San Quentin was hallowed ground for a black man, a revolutionary battlefield where George Jackson was murdered by a CDC sharpshooter. On this site brave black men killed and died to change a system that was uncontrollably and with impunity murderous and brutal toward their kind. But the chilling aspect of this site and prison was that the war was still going on. A guard had been killed just days ago by a projectile fired from a blowgun in the cell block that housed most of the top leaders of the organization George created, the Black Guerrilla Family.

—Flores A. Forbes, *Will You Die With Me?*

The joint, to most outsiders, was purportedly controlled by the governor, the California Department of Corrections, and the prison administrators, with their chow-hall gun cages, gun towers, and blitzkrieg-like cell block searches. But from where I stood, within the joint, control, especially the control of how inmates thought was in question from day one of my arrival. But my political upbringing in the Black Panther Party had prepared me well for the almost concentration-camp theater I was to experience.

I had become a better man because of my association with great minds, including Huey P. Newton, George Jackson, and others. I was exposed to situations that showed me what kind of character it took to be brave and not afraid of life in prison as an invisible man.

The Black Panther Party placed a great deal of significance on the issue of incarceration of black people in general and black men in particular. This was emphasized in point number eight of the BPP's Ten-Point Platform and Program, which was essentially the BPP's business plan. Gleaned from a survey of African American communities in the San Francisco Oakland Bay Area in 1966, by its founders Huey P. Newton and Bobby Seale, the Ten-Point Platform and Program described the primary issues and concerns that many blacks felt were important enough to even use organized force to achieve. Point number eight stated: We want freedom for all black men held in federal, state, county, and city prisons and jails. We believe that all black people should be released from the many jails and prisons because they have not received a fair and impartial trial.

Early on, the notion of going to prison, for me back then, was an abstract thought; it never crossed my mind. When I was actually breaking the law, waging revolution, I never really believed I'd go to prison. On the other hand, as a black man living and growing up in urban America, I had experienced others going to prison on a pretty regular basis. Many friends and comrades had gone to prison, even my uncle Connie Seymour had gone to prison. This persisted in my life up until the very day that I arrived in prison in 1980:

> The joint was different compared to the era of George Jackson, Hugo "Yogi" Pennel, the early BGF and the ethnic prison gangs such as Mexican Mafia, Nuestra Familia and the Aryan Brotherhood. People were rumored to be welded in their cells, inmates were beaten by guards with impunity and murdered, and there were next to no activities that could help you when you got out, that is, if you did. There were indeterminate sentences, so when George Jackson got six months to life for a $70 gas station robbery, he wound up doing ten to fifteen years and never left the joint alive. That was the old California Department of

Corrections in classic form. But it was guys like George Jackson and his crew who changed the way inmates were treated in the CDC. They fought a revolution behind bars and won. They protested, they killed and they died, and that's the reason why the joint changed to a place where you could do your time as a man.

—Flores A. Forbes, *Will You Die With Me?*

H. Bruce Franklin points out in his fabulous book *Prison Writings in 20th Century America* that the voices of prisoners writing about their experiences in American prisons spoke volumes about the savagery of the prison system in America, and the galvanizing effect it had on two men in particular that changed the system via their actions and the written word. According to Franklin, "*The Autobiography of Malcolm X* appeared at a crucial moment in American history. In 1965, the civil rights movement metamorphosed into the black liberation movement." The strategic goal was the same, "Freedom," and Malcolm X, who was formerly incarcerated himself, influenced a new cadre of black activists outside and within the prison system, including Eldridge Cleaver, Huey P. Newton, and a host of others. But the most notable, for his actions and writings, which made a connection from within the prison system in California and expanded to other prison systems throughout the land, including Attica in particular, was the work of George L. Jackson.

Based on my indirect knowledge and my direct experience, I believe that George Jackson was the primary instigator, along with the outside support he engendered, for what became known as the modern prison change movement in the sixties and seventies. George Jackson, from within the prison and often from solitary confinement, declared war on the CDC and demanded his humanity in no uncertain terms and was willing to give his life and to kill if necessary. As Franklin also points out regarding George Jackson, he was "the main spokesman of the movement inside the prison itself." His letters, published as the "Soledad Brother," were read widely by those in prison and outside prison and brought to life his struggle, our struggle, in vivid and personal detail, describing his day-to-day perseverance with a system that sought to kill him and his allies and his spirit but which only succeeded in galvanizing George to enlighten and incite prisoners in California and across the country.

George's writings and his actions as time went by helped to advance a movement to change prison conditions. In 1970, George was one of three black prisoners in Soledad charged with the murder of a white guard, which was viewed by the CDC as retaliation for the shooting deaths of three black inmates at Soledad by a guard tower sharpshooter. They became renowned as the Soledad Three. This case in general, and with special emphasis on George, became a cause célèbre, internationally attracting many high-profile supporters as part of a Soledad Brothers Defense Committee (SBDC). Some of the better-known members of the SBDC were Julian Bond, Marlon Brando, Jane Fonda, Allen Ginsburg, Tom Hayden, Pete

Seeger, and Angela Davis. Later that year, at the urging of California state senator Mervyn Dymally and the California Legislative Black Caucus, and as a response to inquiries and protests led by the SBDC and Angela Davis, an investigation was launched into prisoner treatment at Soledad. This inquiry resulted in several Congressional Hearings by Congress in October 1971. But still, much of the change movement regarding prisoners' rights and their struggle in California was stewarded by George's relationship with the Black Panther Party.

George Jackson and Black Panther Party founder Huey P. Newton were both in the California Department of Corrections in the late sixties but never met. Yet, each saw the other as pivotal to the other's existence, especially with creating a voice for the invisible men both had become. George saw from his many years in prison that the party was the appropriate vehicle to use in fighting against a vicious prison system. And Huey saw the power of George and his actions in changing how the system treated prisoners from the inside.

Probably the most fascinating aspect of the George Jackson legend or myth is how he created, organized, influenced, and sustained the prison change movement from within a prison cell. Yes, he did write a book that sold over 400,000 copies which was read in and outside of prison. The Black Panther Party printed his articles in their weekly newspaper, which had a circulation of over 125,000 copies. And he engendered wide support from celebrities, the masses, and the brothers on the street and in the cell block. But I suspect that a small portion of the change process was done within the prison and as always, this message was sent by kite (a euphemism for a prison letter) to other California prisons and to others around the country, including Attica. Communications between people that are incarcerated still fascinates the public and prison officials. Most of it is done via the circuitous transfer system in the California Department of Corrections with prisoners assigned to carry messages to other inmates in other prisons. Visitors are involved also, and even some lawyers are part of this underground communications network that informs incarcerated people.

But then I believe a larger portion of this change movement within the prison was caused by the organization that George created within the prison. Very little with regard to official knowledge and documentation of the organization he created, that in many ways still exists within California prisons and in many instances on the streets, is known. He was a member of the Black Panther Party to the public and to many in prisons. But the organization named the Black Guerrilla Family, which I heard nothing about until I walked into the CDC, was truly an underground guerrilla organization.

My first encounter with the Black Guerrilla Family occurred when I first arrived in Soledad State Prison. Many, as it turned out, were young black men I had grown up with in Southeast San Diego. I was awestruck at their seriousness under such circumstances and with the daring nature of their struggle in such close quarters against multiple enemies. They had built an organization that had a dual function for the black inmate in that they were the official representative of black men in the CDC and they also provided a protective network for their group—directly and indirectly through the myth of their existence. The group's seriousness was really reflected in one skill that each member was required to learn: Swahili. Following in George Jackson's footsteps, all BGF members were required to learn Swahili so that they could communicate in a language that the guards and other enemies did not know.

But in none of Jackson's writings and interviews was there any mention of the Black Guerrilla Family. In a letter to Angela Davis, he does allude to a dedicated group of black men who are in prison: "Every brother down here is under the influence of the party line. . . . All of these are beautiful brothers, ones who have stepped across the line into the position from which there can be no retreat. All are fully committed." (Jackson, 1970) But in my estimation George Jackson was a true urban guerrilla who had adapted a form of organizing so innovative that within a racist prison system remained invisible until they revealed themselves to the public the day he died.

In August of 1971 George Jackson was killed in a rebellion at San Quentin. Several guards and inmates were also killed. Nine days after his death, all the convicts in New York's Attica State Prison memorialized him in a ceremony described by revolutionary inmate Sam Melville in his posthumous *Letters from Attica*: "At the midday meal, not a man ate or spoke—black, white, brown, red. Many wore black armbands. . . . No one can remember anything like it here before. . . . G. J. was beloved by inmates throughout the country." (Melville, Franklin, 1999)

The Attica Rebellion took place ten days after this demonstration, signaling a climax in the prison change movement in America that still reverberates today.

* * *

"One ever feels his twoness—an American, a Negro; two souls, two thoughts, two reconciled strivings; two warring ideals in one dark body, whose dogged strength alone keeps it from being asunder."

"He simply wishes to make it possible for a man to be both a Negro and an American, without being cursed and spit upon by his fellows, without having the doors of Opportunity closed roughly in his face."

—W. E. B. Du Bois, *The Souls of Black Folk*

The idea, the metaphor, the trope "invisible man" is one we'd do well to remember because it so aptly depicts our history and current condition. It is useful in keeping us sane so we can navigate the culture responsible for its existence. Ellison's metaphor depicted a black, unnamed protagonist in 1952, who demanded that America see him during the Jim Crow era of America in the groundbreaking novel.

The trope about black people being invisible has been used by other black scholars in discussing our being in America. Du Bois was one of the first to focus on black people's presence and survival in post-slavery America. He wrote about us by using an elegant metaphor, which depicted our existence in America as being invisible, on one hand, behind a veil of discrimination from our fellow white citizens and having the ability at a moment of consciousness to unveil our other self for the world to see. His concept of this double consciousness in my estimation was needed as an explanation for us as a people to survive within a country that despised our surviving and not perishing after slavery. We needed this trope to keep our sanity intact in order to navigate an oppressive society long after Emancipation and into the twenty-first century.

The message applies today.

I am writing about black men who are formerly incarcerated, who also exist in today's America and are also demanding to be seen, not in a loud voice, but by their persistent striving to be viewed fairly as people who need an opportunity. They want a second chance to make good on their efforts to survive the stigma of incarceration. We need and demand this favorable recognition, lest we remain in the shadows of fear. For years and, for some of us, decades go by as some formerly incarcerated black men hide behind a self-imposed veil, biding their time and struggling to overcome the obstacles, so that one day they can lift the veil and walk the earth without retribution from the stigma of incarceration.

Today, having successfully reinvented myself as a restored citizen, I believe it is paramount to create a process that helps others and establishes a dialogue with interested and experienced voices, which will alert others that it can be done.

Today, as an associate vice president for Strategic Policy and Program Implementation at Columbia University in the City of New York, I have a general rule that I apply to my professional conduct. It is to be heard and not seen. The biggest problem for the professional black man, or any black man for that matter, is his physical presence in a space that is not accustomed to seeing him. It can be distracting, so much so that his physical presence is blown out of proportion, and when he speaks, his imagined size drowns out his words. This may sound unusual to most people, but let me give a current example of this exaggeration of the black man's presence in space. When Michael Brown was murdered by Darren Wilson, a racist policeman in Ferguson, Missouri, on August 9, 2014, the officer testified to the Grand Jury that Mr. Brown had grown into a ten-foot behemoth right in front of his eyes. Horrified, he just had to use excessive force and bring the brute down. Funny thing about this cartoon description, the Grand Jury believed him. (Ironically, this event happened on the twenty-ninth anniversary of my release from prison.) But going forward, as a black man if what you say is heard, that is a significant accomplishment, as opposed to being seen or perceived as an angry black man who has had opportunities to assimilate but still appears threatening to his colleagues.

Education, skill-set building, and formal training in a profession or trade are the key and foundation for becoming visible in a positive way. Once you have received your training, you need perseverance and patience as a formerly incarcerated black man in order to go knocking from door to door and being rejected more than accepted. Pay attention and learn how to hear the noise of rejection. And pay closer attention to the signals of acceptance and recognition. Appreciate that even when things don't look as if they are going your way, your efforts are paying off. I can't stress this enough because sometimes you are so angry and despondent that your eyes are so clouded, your ears so covered, you don't recognize when a person is acknowledging your value, your gifts, and when they are actually saying: yes.

Most importantly, and I see this as a milestone in your development, create and cultivate your social and professional network. Once you begin, you must know your circle of acquaintances, professional and social. Your relationships, the people you know are going to be pivotal to your success and getting ahead. And do the people you know, know who your other people are so that your engagement with people, even when you are not around, is working for you? During your climb back in to society, you must make every effort to have, cultivate, and nurture strong positive relationships with people you trust and with whom you can communicate. You must build relationships of mutual respect. The education is important but the network is a key to moving through the marketplace successfully. This process never stops. It shouldn't. Today, I am still trying to build and expand my network as part of a group of formerly incarcerated professionals in an attempt to build sustainability in the world of the formerly incarcerated. Nobel Laureate Gary Becker believed that society and commerce missed key talent in their search for the best and brightest when they excluded people who were different or stigmatized by society. Remember: it is to their benefit if you are ready to get down, so break out your business card and network.

Removing the stigma of incarceration externally is a major goal. The work you do via your education and network is important in reaching this goal. But remember the first two pieces to this process, your education and skills building and your network, will make the external stigma easier to remove. Moreover, the work of removing the internal stigma begins and ends with how you think and feel about yourself. Know thyself and everybody else will come clearly into your view. You'll better understand who they are. You want people to see your true character and personality before they can reduce you to a category: formerly incarcerated. Then, the doors in your personal and professional life will open. The mental health work is the hard personal work you must do. You must defeat and overcome the fear many of us have of seeing a mental health professional. You are stronger for asking for help and taking the help. You are weaker walking around with a treatable disorder that is the result of the close-quarter oppression you may have faced in prison. Let's call it what it is: post-traumatic stress disorder. Let's also face the fact that living as a black man in America is a traumatic experience. And this can also become more stressful if you have been to prison. It takes work and patience, but put in the effort to talk to mental health care professionals, get yourself evaluated, and come out, even if you don't think you have a problem. You won't be wasting your time.

Telling my story in a book helped me do a few things: first, I was able to frame eighteen years of experience that I could not put on a résumé, and second, I was able to work through my demons and issues. Writing might work for you as well. You don't have to publish it or even let another person read it. Then again, sharing what you've worked out on paper with someone in your circles—family, friends, and colleagues—might go a long way toward your healing and a better quality of life. Some people have written poems about their lives that are non-traditional, and some have just written their stories in a personal journal that they only share with loved ones. I decided that I would write a memoir and get it published. That was the easy part, but the most difficult was going on a book tour and doing the publicity that would force me to face the public, as many were very critical of my story, but nonetheless, I had to do it and eradicate that final demon lurking in my life. Many may find other ways to exorcise these fears, like organizing a 111th Street Group and talking about it out loud in a group with the same issues.

The most important step for a successful, formerly incarcerated person, especially a black man, is to get comfortable telling your story. Once you've achieved that step, share yourself with someone like you, mentor someone, and become a friend to those who have been down the same road.

*   *   *

I have always found books an intriguing way to find knowledge. First, as a young person growing up in San Diego, California, my siblings and I spent hours reading books we borrowed from the local book mobile. And then I found the revolution in the books my brother used to bring home from college while he was a student at the University of California at Los Angeles. The most intriguing was *The Crisis of the Negro Intellectual*, by Harold Cruse. Then in the Black Panther Party, I was usually the first person in the class and sat in the front row at our weekly political education class. We read some great books during those classes like *Wretched of the Earth*, by Frantz Fanon. The focus in these classes was reading for political education and analyzing the information in the texts and assessing how it might guide us and help in our struggle.

But the most enjoyable reading experience I had was in prison. Maybe because of my life journey, I was paying closer attention to the words as I was still searching for information that would guide me and help me once I was released. There was a treasure trove of books in the prison library at Soledad State Prison in Salinas, California. But nothing could compare to English 175, Masterpieces of American Literature, a class taught by professor Robin Brooks from the San José State University prison college program.

What made this class so enjoyable as an intellectual experience was the beginning of the course. The first thing that Professor Brooks said was I am going to teach you how to read not just for leisure and enjoyment but I will teach you how to be critical of the literature and what these books might mean to you as a person. He said the American novel evolved as a vehicle that could convey the true story of this country, with all of its supposed glory and its warts and all, including slavery and the mistreatment of the native people over the years. He introduced us to deconstructionism. Basically, you can read and analyze a text, and the results of what you think you have read may not be the same as someone else's. Or put another way, there may be multiple interpretations of what the story means to each member of the class.

The other teaching tool he gave us was the journal. We had to read and analyze each book, short story, or poem and write our analysis about each assignment in this journal. I still have mine today. We read *The Scarlet Letter*, by Nathaniel Hawthorne; *Bartleby the Scrivener: A Story of Wall Street*, by Herman Melville; and the Melville book *Benito Cereno*. I especially loved the character Babo, the leader of the slave rebellion. Walt Whitman's *A Song of Myself* was also part of the syllabus. And Mark Twain's *Huckleberry Finn*, which caused some tension. Those goddamn Aryan Brotherhood guys loved reading this out loud, placing special emphasis on their enunciation of each word "nigger" when it appeared in the text. I think that's about one hundred times.

There was the poetry of Emily Dickinson, number 185 to number 280, and "The Awakening," by Kate Chopin. Edith Wharton's really dull *The Age of Innocence* and T. S. Eliot's "The Love Song of J. Alfred Prufrock." We read and analyzed Robert Frost and Sylvia Platt, and I really got a charge out of *The Great Gatsby*, by F. Scott Fitzgerald. But he saved the best for last as professor Brooks professed that he thought the best American novel was *Invisible Man*, by Ralph Ellison. Man, did those Nazis hate that he said that. *Invisible Man* is my all-time favorite. I read it with deep intent, as I carried that intellectual intensity with me until I was released.

So around 2014 when I read *The Count of Monte Cristo*, I knew I had found something. I searched deeper and found that Dumas was of African descent and that much of the imagery surrounding the story is in tribute to his black father who was a persecuted general in Napoleon's Army. I knew I had found another gem that I could learn from and teach to my persecuted brothers.

It is, in my estimation, the most powerful story of a man going to prison and fighting against tremendous odds to remove the stigma of incarceration once he is free. This tale by Alexandre Dumas, *The Count of Monte Cristo*, is a book I recommend highly to all formerly incarcerated people and especially to their family, friends, and their network.

The Count of Monte Cristo

"Wait and hope."
—Alexandre Dumas, *The Count of Monte Cristo*

"Wait and hope" is a line from Alexandre Dumas's classic novel *The Count of Monte Cristo*. The story is about the trials, tribulations, and triumphs of one Edmond Dantés during the Napoleonic era in France. What resonates with me is that it's a tale about a man who goes to prison and overcomes the greatest of obstacles and in many ways mirrors the Bruce Western prescription—education/skills, social network, and removing the stigma of incarceration—that a black man must follow in order to become successful in the United States following a prison term.

Every person, in general, at some point in their life is searching for that magic pill or "genie in the bottle" that will make them acceptable, rich, famous, and outstanding in the field of their choice. But those of us who were formerly incarcerated just want to survive. We want to not feel like we are hunted at every turn with the threat of being returned to prison hanging over our head. Stories have power. They can give us a little fuel to keep going. Like music.

This classic tale begins with the protagonist, Edmond Dantés, being framed and sent to prison for allegedly aiding the return of Napoleon Bonaparte from exile and back into power in 1814. While in prison, he meets Abbé Faria, who educates him on the ways of the world and enlightens him about his false hopes of being freed because he is really innocent. The two hatch a plan to escape, but the Abbé dies before both can flee. Dantès makes good his escape in the Abbé's burial sack and is tossed into the Mediterranean to freedom. However, the key to Dantès's success after taking flight was provided by the Abbé in the form of a treasure map, which leads him to a vault full of gold on the island of Monte Cristo. Once free and wealthy because of the treasure, Dantès organizes his life to return to France and take revenge against those who have framed him. But Dantès has undergone a miraculous transformation. He has been educated and understands the world through a sophisticated perspective, and the riches he now controls have aided him in organizing and developing a network of collaborators, who assist him in taking his revenge. Moreover, he has acquired the ability to dissemble, and the transforming imagery, as manifested in his fourteen years in prison, has helped him to remove the stigma of incarceration. The imagery of this erasure is alluded to in a scene after his escape when Dantès shaves his beard off, and when he looks into the mirror at his clean-shaven face, he no longer recognizes the prisoner he once was. Likewise, his reinvention is so complete that when he returns to the mainland of France, his enemies and loved ones no longer can recognize him as Edmond Dantès. He has been transformed into the Count of Monte Cristo.

CHAPTER 12

What We Need

"Point number eight: We want freedom for all black men held in federal, state, county, and city prisons and jails. We believe that all black people should be released from the many jails and prisons because they have not received a fair and impartial trial.

"Point number nine: We want all black people when brought to trial to be tried in court by a jury of their peer group or people from their black communities, as defined by the Constitution of the United States. We believe that the courts should follow the United States Constitution so that black people will receive fair trials. The Fourteenth Amendment of the United States Constitution gives a man a right to be tried by his peer group. A peer group is a person from a similar economic, social, religious, geographical, environmental, historical and racial background. To do this the court will be forced to select a jury from the black community from which the black defendant came. We have been, and are being, tried by all-white juries that have no understanding of the 'average reasoning man' of the black community."—Points eight and nine of the Ten-Point Platform and Program of the Black Panther Party, October 15, 1966

What we want and what we believe are the beginning words on each of the policy statements that became the Black Panther Party's Ten-Point Platform and Program. These statements were taken from a survey conducted in the black communities in the San Francisco Oakland Bay Area in 1966. Of the ten, only points eight and nine focus on hyper-incarceration as a major issue for black people at that time. However, point seven was the most problematic and pressing, as it dealt with police brutality and the murder of black people.

Growing up in the Black Panther Party, I believed in these two policy statements and worked in a program that we hoped would help prisoners inside and prepare them for their eventual release. The program was called the Free Busing to Prison Program. The program provided free transportation by bus to prisons for black and poor people in various cities throughout the United States. Most of the prisons and the men incarcerated in them in this country are hundreds of miles away from the loved ones of many inmates. We believed it was important to these invisible men and their well-being to make it possible for their loved ones to visit, even though they were shuttered away from the public.

When I was in prison, I remember visiting day as a bright and shining day. All of the prisoners put on their best pair of jeans and a nicely starched blue shirt with buffed shoes. It was just like going on a date, or for some, going to church in their Sunday best. It was a time to relax. If you had long hair and it was braided, you would undo your cornrows so that your woman could braid your hair while you talked.

But what is amazing to me today as I reflect on my journey is the quality of people, mostly black men, who came out of prison, as they are some of the most remarkable human beings. I am proud to call them my fellow travelers. These fellow travelers, who in many ways set the tone for invisible men coming home, are some of the most outstanding individuals in our history as a people in America.

Fellow Travelers

"Malcolm X had a special meaning for black convicts. A former prisoner himself, he had risen from the lowest depths to great heights. For this reason he was a symbol of hope, a model for thousands of black convicts who found themselves trapped in the vicious PPP cycle: prison-parole-prison. One thing that the judges, policemen and administrators of prisons seem never to have understood and for which they certainly do not make allowances, is that Negro convicts, basically, rather than see themselves as criminals and perpetrators of misdeeds, look upon themselves as prisoners of war, the victims of a vicious, dog-eat-dog social system that is so heinous as to cancel out their own malefactions: in the jungle there is no right or wrong."

—Eldridge Cleaver, *Soul on Ice*

The Eldridge Cleaver passage from his best-selling memoir *Soul on Ice* is a statement from his soul that most black men who have been to prison would concur with, as I certainly did. There is not one black man, regardless of his religious or nonreligious belief, who has been imprisoned in America since the publication of the *Autobiography of Malcolm X* in 1965, who has not read it and taken his story as the bible for conduct when one leaves prison.

Nevertheless, most of us may have desired to emulate his story of reinvention, but only a few have aspired to the letter of his lofty cause to liberate black people in America.

When Eldridge left prison, he became a revolutionary. George Jackson became a revolutionary in prison but never left alive. Chester Himes left prison and became a great writer of hilarious but dark ghetto humor with his classic crime novels featuring two black New York City police detectives, Gravedigger Jones and Coffin Ed Johnson. Charles Dutton became a revolutionary in prison, and when he left, he became a Tony Award–winning stage actor. Etheridge Knight left prison, where he honed his writing skills, and became a well-regarded poet and academic. Jeff Henderson learned to cook in the joint and now, as a formerly incarcerated person, is a celebrity chef. And there are many more who have transformed themselves once leaving prison.

Most black men who have been to prison probably believed something similar to what Cleaver articulated in 1968, that they did not get a fair break in life and that the "prisoner of war" moniker reflects a belief on the factual injustice they live under and for the environment of white supremacy that their crimes were committed in. Or some, like me, believed whatever their role or goal in society was that their actions were political in nature and thus they were urban political prisoners of some sort. The adage that if you cannot do the time, do not commit the crime rings irrelevant in the joint, as many will tell you they do not respect the United States criminal justice system on its face. Unlike many of the brothers I encountered in prison, my brief stint in prison was preceded by a life as a revolutionary studying Malcolm, Eldridge, Huey P. Newton, and others. So when I arrived, I was already a converted soul to the cause of change. I came to prison a true believer, understanding that we were at war and that surviving inside with a goal of becoming a change agent for the brothers was paramount on my mind. Huey P. Newton used to tell me that in America the revolutionary organizations created by black people will always be destroyed but what is acutely important for the individual surviving member is how he or she adapts to this misfortune. He says as survivors they must acclimate into society as change agents carrying the same belief system they believed in as revolutionaries within the organization.

Malcolm's journey began on the mean streets of urban America, but unlike some black men who come to prison, he also possessed a powerful tool as manifested in his street knowledge and reinforced with a strong curiosity about life and how to survive. These skills served him well, as they obviously enhanced his critical thinking and personal assessment when he decided to reinvent himself. Almost every black man who is in prison, and even those who are not and have never seen the inside of the penal colony, fantasizes about coming to the joint as a hustler and a gangster, which is supposed to aid your transformation into a revolutionary, a more robust accomplishment. This is also reflected in the basic prison reading material that is passed around the joint between black inmates, like the novels of Iceberg Slim and Donald Goines who wrote about the life in prison and on the streets as dashing, two-gunned hoods with pretty women hanging on both arms and pockets full of money. On the other hand, some do transform and convert, as revealed in the real-life metamorphosis of Iceberg Slim, who aspired to become a revolutionary at some point in prison and acted upon this new belief once released and out of the pimp game years later.

Likewise, the story of Malcolm's detailed studying of the Webster dictionary is prison lore as we all had well-turned dictionaries. In black urban satire this is portrayed in black comedic sketches, as in Keenan Ivory Wayans's hit variety show *In Living Color*, where streetwise ex-cons use fifty-cent words that usually do not mean what the definition states. But where Malcolm's journey differs from most, and I draw some similar parallels in my life, is that he educated himself in prison, and, unlike most, he established a powerful network that connected with him in the joint and facilitated a safe landing through his well-documented career as the national minister of the Nation of Islam, followed by his heroic turn as the "black prince" of the civil rights movement.

Malcolm's life journey represents many things to black America in general, but in particular, it became somewhat of a disconcerting urban myth with a disjointed meaning to young and mature black men who embraced his way of life. They promoted that going to prison for many young black men is a rite of passage to be worn as a badge of honor that one proudly admits to in one's inner circle and shouts to the world. Today, you can hear this in an urban toast that becomes a spellbinding lyric in a rap song or spoken-word skit. Although I believe he would not have intended this belief system, as stated above, Malcolm did, in my estimation, through his ministry and his deep and revealing story, remove the stigma of incarceration. This is true for many who followed him into the Nation of Islam, but for some, they do not choose to shout their status to the outside world that sees incarceration as a stigma.

* * *

Surely the incarcerated need more than visits and role models before leaving the joint so that they can stay free. They do need family and friends, loved ones and lovers. But once they get out and begin their reentry, they will also need their new coworkers and colleagues to connect with their need to relate and socialize as part of a network. They will need this to assure personally that they do have a future in the outside world. The public-policy and administration apparatus also needs to connect with these returning citizens and make that second-chance commitment that former president Bush mentioned in his State of the Union address a reality. The returning citizen must also do his part and get that education, professional/trade development, as they strive to remove the stigma of external and internal incarceration. But it is the sum of all of these parts that needs to happen and make this a reality, like a real capital investment. An investment needs to come from both sides to make those of us coming out truly visible men.

Capital Investment

"White supremacy is the conscious or unconscious belief or the investment in the inherent superiority of some, while others are believed to be innately inferior. And it doesn't demand the individual participation of the singular bigot. It is a machine operating in Perpetuity, because it doesn't demand that somebody be in place driving."

—Michael Eric Dyson

I have heard many public-policy wonks and policy makers, so-called black conservatives and other social critics rant and rave about what they think is needed to solve certain problems in our inner cities in general, and with young black males in particular, especially the ones who are encumbered by the criminal justice system. Well, I would like to say this to them. I have experienced what they will have to go through in order for them to assimilate into this society. And having experienced this, I can honestly say, there are many parts of this society that are not really serious about letting us back in as fully restored citizens. My getting back from the social deficit of being in prison should not be an exception. And from what I've seen of the so-called initiatives, proposals, and programs that are supposed to help them, they can't possibly work, unless there is a real push from the other side of society that dishonestly promotes the so-called level playing field.

The biggest reason for them not being able to work is the assumption that all of these programs are developed from, which basically is that we all have a level playing field to participate in this society—a second chance. You know, it's like all of a sudden everything in this society is even and everyone that is affected is told to shut up because the past is the past and the twain shall not meet again. Okay, let's have three hundred to four hundred years of slavery, Black Codes, Jim Crow, and on the carceral equivalent, convict leasing, chain gangs, and state and private prison industries with slave wages. And then let's stop this only on paper in 1954 with the *Brown* Supreme Court decision and subsequent civil rights legislation. Now, we will work with you up to a point, but remember the stuff done to you from day one is not our fault and the rules say if you bring it up, that you will be labeled lazy, a crybaby, good-for-nothing, a liberal's bastard child, a detriment to your community, or someone who just didn't take advantage of the crumbs we gave you. Even though we believe in the Founding Fathers and their Constitution, we don't accept responsibility for how they really treated your people—back in the day. That's not our fault. However, after thirty or so years of affirmative action, we must stop this remedial action because you might get ahead. (The previous three hundred to four hundred years and counting have and continue to be affirmative action for white people in general and white men in particular.) We can no longer allow you to get ahead of good, decent, solid, white folks just because of a little slavery, segregation, and so what if we continue to deny you your rights. Go get a job nigger, there's plenty of them out there you know, in the NBA, NFL, or at the post office.

The National Basketball Association and the National Football League are talent driven, but the due diligence would make it very difficult for someone with a record to get one of those coveted jobs. On the other hand, the post office is a big problem, since they have the Box prominently displayed which will affect blacks who were formerly incarcerated (US Post Office application, in the Other Information section, question 7a). But the level-playing-field advocates say we can't do this because it discriminates against white folks and that's a violation of our constitutional rights under the Fourteenth and Fifteenth Amendments. (Yeah, right!) So this is their argument in a nutshell, and it sounds pretty silly to me, coming from these black and white conservatives who no longer believe it makes sense for an intelligent man or women to define their own situation and not accept the dishonest narrative about this country being a fair and level playing field for all. Especially for those who have served their time and assume that this society is really giving them a second chance. As Malcolm X pointed out, you've been had, hoodwinked, bamboozled, or railroaded by this dishonest narrative, which controls the airwaves.

Nonetheless, for there to be a "piss of a chance" at making it in this society, young brothers and other folks like me need an infusion that is simply a type of "capital invest-ment." People succeed in this country because they receive that capital investment at some point in their life. It's a quality input from a parent or mentor. (Luckily, I have had both.) It's the opportunity to receive the education and training that can help you to develop a respectable livelihood in this society, which could mean an infusion of money to help defray the cost. And then society must be responsible for their part.

The proposition for the capital investment is for the full weight of society to be engaged in solving this issue, much like the effort put forth after World War II and the Marshall Plan. This includes its public-policy apparatus, the private and civil sectors, and a small capital infusion to get behind a new paradigm that will work jointly with the formerly incarcerated at removing the stigma of incar-ceration, a stain that society impugns upon the formerly incarcerated for life. If this happens, then and only then I believe we can seriously reduce the issue of recidivism which is the real precursor to criminal justice reform. Work with us and do not look upon us as lepers.

On the other hand, people getting out of prison (if they do) have an obligation to work at rehabilitating themselves, too. It must start with the formerly incarcerated and his or her efforts at building, planning, and implementing their new life once they are on the outside. However, society must be responsible for its part by accepting the concept of rehabilita-tion. So there must be a meeting that takes place halfway on the issue of rehabilitation and assimilation into society.

Society is not there yet and neither are most of the individuals rejecting society because of their refusal to acclimate. I don't think the average brother coming out of the joint really trusts this society, and the feeling is obviously mutual. But as someone who has been on the other side of the wall, it's very inviting if you see "a will and a way" to get back into society being offered to you. Why, just look at any job application and that question that removes you from any hope of getting your foot in the door, even if you are qualified: Have you ever been convicted of a crime? And sometimes it's split up into two parts, and they refer specifically to a felony or misdemeanor. And some of the applications ask for a time frame, like has this conviction occurred within the last seven years or ten years, etc. This question nullifies you automatically to the employer, and conversely, it has a nullifying and impactful effect on the formerly incarcerated applicant. Moreover, it is not just about banning the Box, because banning the Box does not remove the doubt, mistrust, or prejudice of the hiring manager who is reviewing the application. The hiring manager in most cases has been instilled with their value judgment, which includes stigmatizing the formerly incarcerated, the poor, people with different names, and people of color.

Nevertheless, the external stigma of going to prison or being formerly incarcerated will never go away. That is, until we meet halfway. Every society has needed prisons, but most societies don't know what to do with those people who go to prison and eventually get out. I have been to prison, and I met some people there that convinced me that there definitely is a need for prisons. But being black in this society and going to prison almost washes you out of society for the rest of your life. You become anathema, and this can't change until the former prisoner who becomes a restored citizen and society as the jailor begin to understand that they're in this together.

The marketplace of ideas and practice that currently promote a concept similar to a capital investment to assist the formerly incarcerated in general, and black men who were formerly incarcerated in particular, is complex and varied, and even though progress is being made, there still remain many obstacles to overcome going forward.

Many universities and nonprofits are doing great work in this space, as well as many public officials that are closely aligned with the private sector, to create more and diverse opportunities that will assist in removing the stigma of incarceration. However, a significant aspect in activating the concept of the capital investment is manifested in recognizing those formerly incarcerated professionals working in this space who are well trained and who also provide a wealth of personal experience and knowledge about the work, which can help bring about real criminal justice reform in the final analysis. But there is still much doubt from our partners with seeing this relationship to fruition.

On one side, there are those of us working to redeem ourselves by jumping through the societal hoops that still remain. Do this and that and you will be accepted and not tainted. Moreover, what if those doing the judging have yet to put in their work so that they can fully appreciate the other side and what we still must overcome? For example, many of my colleagues at Columbia University are doing great work in this area via the Center for Justice and in other areas of the university. On this one occasion, my colleagues were organizing a forum that would explore the feasibility and rationale behind a reduced-bail policy for young offenders in general, but with a specific focus on nonviolent offenders. This program was being done in collaboration with a local politician who wanted to give exposure to a bill he was submitting to the legislative body he served on.

The panel was organized with five or six experts, and amongst this group one of the experts was a formerly incarcerated professional. When the local politician was told of the composition of the panel, his people raised an issue about the formerly incarcerated person who was proposed for the panel. They asked what he was convicted of and how much time he had done. This particular formerly incarcerated professional was a vice president in a well-regarded reentry company and was well on his way to receiving his doctorate from a prominent university. They said they wanted to get another person of their choice. My colleagues held fast, but the politician and his staff, as far as I could see, did not believe that the subject matter could be discussed and presented by a diverse group of experts, which included most notably an expert who had direct experience with the subject matter. (Many of the experts involved in the discussion around criminal justice reform are formerly incarcerated professionals with impeccable academic credentials.) This particular politician is in need of that capital investment overhaul that many policy makers must experience when they do not believe that the knowledge of a formerly incarcerated professional is relevant to the cause or issue. The system in my opinion will never change if this one-sided thinking persists when tackling criminal justice reform. The stigma label is loud and clear in this case.

Moreover, some community residents who live in high-impact areas that have an unusually large number of people returning to their community from prison are also not interested in making a human capital investment with regard to meeting these returning citizens halfway. I was attending a community planning board meeting in Harlem and a local reentry group was making a presentation that focused on them locating a halfway house in the neighborhood. I heard some of the black people present shouting at the top of their voices, "We don't want any more criminals coming into our community. Send them somewhere else." Many people were silent, and I wondered if that silence was recognition that the naysayers to the half-way house may have been talking about someone's son, brother, husband, or father returning to their community but unwanted by their neighbors.

Conclusions and Suggestions

"Three powerful forces interacted. The first is a psychology of American race relations characterized by stereotypes of black criminals, unconscious preferences for whiteness over blackness and the lack of empathy among whites for black offenders and their families. The second, which shaped the first, is a three-centuries-old pattern of economic, political and social dominance of blacks by whites. The third, enabled by the first two, is the Republican Southern Strategy of appealing to racial enmities and anxieties by use of seemingly neutral code words."

—Michael Tonry, *Punishing Race: A Continuing American Dilemma*

The focus of my narrative is clearly to target, enlighten, and educate incarcerated and formerly incarcerated black men, their families, and loved ones and to place the issue of our plight on the public agenda. Those affected black men are the only reason I would out myself like this, especially after thirty years. To shine a light on their plight and to bring attention to the real oppression that affects us externally and internally. However, I do believe that to propose any kind of programmatic solution to this issue of serious reentry for the formerly incarcerated, the affected audience is much broader and diverse. It includes the over sixty million people in America who are traversing the streets with at least a felony conviction on their record.

If a real and productive dialogue is to take place about reentry for the currently incarcerated and the formerly incarcerated, three major issues must be on the agenda: the exception clause of the Thirteenth Amendment; the Box as it relates to employment and university and college admissions; and white supremacy.

First, I have no reason to believe that proposing to amend the Thirteenth Amendment's exception clause, which makes someone convicted of a felony and sent to prison a slave, is even relevant. (The 150th anniversary of the amendment was just celebrated, and there was no mention of the exception clause.) But I do believe there needs to be recognition of this clause and its consequences and how it constitutionally affirms the mistreatment of women and men in federal, state, and local prisons and jails. And this is compounded with the advent of contemporary convict-leasing programs that masquerade as private prisons. I see this especially when it involves black people as the continuation of convict leasing, Black Codes, and Jim Crow as part and parcel of the loophole that is the exception clause of the Thirteenth Amendment. And this continues with the long tail of parole following you around making it difficult for you to gain and restore your rights, especially in the former slave states of the South.

Second, the Box should be banned on all employment applications and on university and college applications. The Box on employment applications should be banned, but not without extensive education and cultural sensitivity training in human resource departments across all industries in the civic, public, and private sectors. The notion that you do not have to self-declare until you are offered the job is very deceptive. Especially since a background check will possibly take place following the hiring letter. This assumes that those in the human resource departments are not prejudiced or are just fabulous and value-free in their judgments. If this is the new thing called "a second chance," what kind of retraining or education will the staff charged with making these changes get? I spoke to a human resource person at a major university who said they do have a screening process but will only ask the screener if there is a red flag after an offer is made. Okay, what happens then? And just to add to this suggestion regarding the Box, a study that was previously noted, done by Devah Pager from Harvard University, showed even if a black man had a degree and no felony conviction, it was more likely for the white applicant with a felony conviction to get the callback for the job.

The Box is also used on many university and college applications and now let me tell you a story about someone's experience with regard to this. I am outing only myself at this writing, so the person whose story this is will remain anonymous. This is the story of a black man who was an outstanding individual from the Midwest. He was so talented that he matriculated at one of this country's elite service academies. After graduation he served in another elite military service unit with distinction. He finished his service and went into the private sector. Made a mistake, got caught, and went to prison. He was released and continued his education, applying to highly selective graduate programs. One such school, in the South, said he could not be accepted into one of their graduate programs because he had been honest and checked the Box. However, another university was a little more enlightened and accepted him. Today, he is an outstanding professor at a liberal arts college. Just think: just because he self-declared on the Box, one school almost prohibited the best person for the job from getting a second chance. That is why the Box needs to go, but with conditions related to human resource retraining.

And finally, a real discussion, warts and all, needs to be convened, not just about race, but about that humongous elephant that is in the room: white supremacy. Yes, that is white supremacy, which is as old as the US Constitution simply because the framers of that document are the original white supremacists of this land. Not those guys running around with sheets covering their bodies. If this is not on the table, we will never remove the true cause for the problem I am discussing. It manifests itself in our current prison system and determines why the formerly incarcerated are treated the way they are. It is manifested in our policing practice of occupying the territory of communities of color. The color of the policeman is irrelevant, so just remember "Gloves" Davis, the machine-gun-wielding policeman who murdered Fred Hampton, was a very dark-skinned black man. White supremacy engendered every plan that was devised to get rid of the niggers since Emancipation and is the bane of every white politician's existence. I am sure that every white politician in this country thought they had a chance to be president of the United States before a black man took the job that all white people believed was reserved for one of their kind. By getting elected president, Barack Obama tipped white supremacy on its head. That, in and of itself, reveals what is the classic definition of white supremacy. It is the reason a compromise was worked out in 1865 between Congress and Abraham Lincoln: the exception clause to the Thirteenth Amendment.

*   *   *

Around 2007, I was invited to give the Howard Thurman Lecture at Stetson University. I was invited by Dr. Jefferson Rogers, the founder of the lecture series. As I was to discover, Dr. Rogers was to provide me with more than just a forum to discuss my book *Will You Die With Me? My Life and the Black Panther Party.* He told me about a plan in close confidence that he and several other academics, advocates, and businessmen were working on. Today, almost a year after his passing, I see this plan in many ways similar to the treasure map that Abbé Faria passed on to Edmond Dantès just before he died in *The Count of Monte Cristo.*

Dr. Rogers was part of a group that had devised a plan to assist the formerly incarcerated with their reentry into society. The plan was premised on the Clinton administration strategy that became his Welfare to Work legislation. The most notable of the academics that Dr. Rogers revealed to me was a Harvard professor named Bruce Western, who had done some groundbreaking research in this space. In hushed tones, he explained the basics of the plan. When a person was released, they would receive a set amount of benefits for reentry and support that would last for five years. They included Section 8 vouchers for housing if needed. They would also receive vouchers for education and skills training in a trade of their choice and a living wage in the form of a stipend. The project would be funded by a federal grant as a pilot for about $2 billion. After I returned from Florida, he kept in touch, even sending a giant loose-leaf binder with the plan details. I unfortunately did not follow up on the group's idea until this writing.

Therefore, I would propose a plan building on the thinking of Dr. Jefferson Rogers and his colleagues that would provide some of the returning citizens' relief and support with their reentry efforts.

First, the amount of money allocated to incarcerate a person, let's assume $31,286 per year (an estimated average by the Vera Institute), would be appropriated to each formerly incarcerated person that is selected to be in the program. When I was released from prison in 1985, the state gave me $200.00. I believe that is the same amount given today to released prisoners in California. For example, if the cost to confine someone was $31,286 per year, the individual would receive that amount annually for up to five years or until they have secured a job with a living wage or are matriculating in an institution of higher learning. Additionally, these same resources would be used to pay for housing, or in the same amount of a Section 8 voucher, training costs, education cost, health care, including mental health if needed, and a stipend. The cost to provide this assistance is more robust because in the calculation of the cost to incarcerate an individual, the majority of the money is used for security, control, and confinement.

Expanding on this model, I would also propose the creation and development of a lobbying plan and strategy that would be representative and work on behalf of the formerly incarcerated in America. And because of their special situation, I would develop a black and Latino caucus to target the needs of these overly oppressed groups. This "mouthpiece project" would focus on current and new public-policy issues that affect this population. I would also propose an entity that would be connected to this project that would become a "think tank." The sole purpose of this group would be to research ideas on how to make reentry into society a more just cause. The startup costs of this operation would come initially from a philanthropic source with a goal of identifying the sixty million or more formerly incarcerated in this country. Once these individuals have been identified and placed on the database, they will be charged dues to join and those funds will defray the cost of the operation going forward.

The overall goal of the group will be to assist each member with removing the stigma of incarceration externally and internally, thus restoring them to full citizenship within the United States, and thus making the term for the group labeled "formerly incarcerated" a special-interest group.